The New Wine is Better

The New Wine is Better

Robert Thom

Whitaker House

THE NEW WINE IS BETTER

Contact Information:
Drummond Thom
Deeper Life Ministries International
P.O. Box 33066
Lousville, KY 40232
Phone: 502.968.2102
e-mail: dlcc@adept.net
web site: www.drummondthom.org

ISBN: 0-88368-036-X
Printed in the United States of America
© 1974 by Drummond Thom

Whitaker House
30 Hunt Valley Circle
New Kensington, PA 15068

Special Printing for Drummond Thom and
Deeper Life Ministries, 2002

Dedication

To my children and my late wife

Beloved wife
Joyce Thom

Children
Drummond Thom
Lionel Thom
Roy Thom
Elaine Thom Greeff
Robert Thom
David Thom
Leonard Thom
Robyn Thom Rodgers

CONTENTS

FOREWORD

The Christian Broacasting Network program, "The 700 Club," was well under way in our Dallas studio when my next guest was introduced and took a seat in front of the television cameras. You might imagine my surprise when the guest, without a word of greeting, raised one hand toward heaven in front of our nationwide audience and boomed forth in his stentorian voice, "The Lord has just shown me a vision—your next station will be in Seattle, Washington!"

If my guest had been anyone else but Robert Thom of South Africa, I would have dismissed this outburst as a publicity gimmick. But this was the man who, at a meeting in Virginia, had correctly predicted three days before the event that Senator Robert Kennedy would be struck down. When the word was spoken about the new television station, I listened intently.

I wasn't too surprised, therefore, when just a week before receiving a copy of *The New Wine Is Better*, I sat in the office of the owner of a television station where I signed a contract to purchase his facilities. That's right—in Seattle, Washington—less than four months after Robert Thom's remarkable prophecy!

The New Wine Is Better is the exciting story of how Jesus Christ transformed a tough, alcoholic seaman from South Africa into a true New Testament man of faith. We have here a thoroughly believable account of a modern day miracle. Its true beauty lies in the fact that it gives glory to Jesus Christ.

9

Some people feel that a true man of faith must go about with a far-away, heavenly expression in his eyes, speaking of such other-worldly things as guidance, revelation, and spirituality. The Apostle Paul thought otherwise, however, when he wrote, "We have this treasure in earthen vessels."

In Robert Thom we have a merger of the authentic heavenly treasure and an authentic earthen vessel. The story of how the two got together makes very interesting reading.

Pat Robertson, President
The Christian Broadcasting Network, Inc.

PREFACE

This is the simple story of how I—one of the most unlikely persons in the world—discovered the power of faith.

Often I have felt like the father in the Bible who said to Jesus, "Lord, I believe; help thou mine unbelief" (Mark 9:24). I am fully aware that whatever faith I have was given to me by Him.

The story is far from complete. So many miraculous things have happened that I hardly knew where to begin—or where to stop. But "these are written that ye might believe" that God truly does respond to simple faith, even today.

In order to protect the confidences of some, a few fictitious names have been used. But the story is true. May it bring glory to the wonderful name of Jesus.

Robert Thom

Introduction

As I travel the world ministering the Gospel, all I get are good reports concerning this book, *The New Wine is Better*. This is the life story of my dad, Robert Thom, whom God raised up and used for his glory.

He was not always a man God used. My dad was an alcoholic until the day of his conversion when Jesus Christ came into his heart and set him totally free. The inspiration of this book and what God did for him has touched the hearts of thousands as they have seen a man of faith who moved under the prophetic anointing and, as a result, saw many needs met.

In the early days, there were times he had to pray in the rent and food. At othert times he had to believe God to provide for us to put gas in the car. Those were the lean years, but they were good years because faith always touches the heart of God and brings change. "For with God nothing shall be impossible" (Luke 1:37).

My dad, Robert Thom, was a man of faith who believed God would do what He had said. I was there; I saw his faith as God provided for all of us and for the ministry He had called dad to do.

This little book will inspire you as it has thousands before you. If God did all these things for Robert Thom, He can do them for you.

Drummond R. Thom

CHAPTER ONE

POOR LITTLE RICH BOY

My name is Robert Thom, and I'm a living miracle; yet I'm just a very ordinary person who has discovered that life doesn't need to be a dumb humdrum of doing the same old things in the same old way, day in and day out . . . not if you're willing to take the risk of living by faith.

Take this $2,000 check, for instance. Would you believe that a man just *handed* this to me, no strings attached? It happened just a few days ago. I was staying at the Travelodge Motel in Zanesville, Ohio. As soon as I awakened that morning, I began to think about my bills. Two thousand dollars is a lot of money when you don't have it. But our printing operation over in Africa needed at least that much just to get off the ground. I'd written about thirty inspirational books for Afrikaans-speaking Christians. The plates had already been made, the paper had been received, and the press was ready to roll. But I had no idea where the money was coming from to pay the employees.

"If I'm going to have enough to pay those workers," I said to God that morning, "You're going to have to perform a two-thousand-dollar miracle for me."

"*Haven't I always taken care of you before?*" He seemed to say.

"Oh, sure," I replied. "I just thought I'd mention it. . . ."

"Then why don't you start praising Me?" the Voice reproved gently. Immediately I remembered that passage in Psalm 22:3 where David spoke of God as the One Who inhabits the praises of Israel.

"Why not?" I asked myself. "I don't have the $2,000, but I've got God's promises; so I'll just take the day off and praise Him."

Arising from my knees, I walked across the room and locked the door. I smiled to myself at what I was about to do. "Whoever heard of taking a day off to praise the Lord?" I chuckled.

I was sure it would be an uplifting experience, however; so I began enthusiastically: "Father, I thank You for supplying all I need. I bless Your Name for this $2,000 that You're going to send me. I praise You that I won't have to send out any begging letters to my friends. Praise the Lord! Hallelujah!"

I paced the floor of that motel room, just rejoicing in Him. The more I praised Him, the smaller that $2,000 seemed! I began to think of many other great things God had done for me. I remembered how He had saved me and changed me so completely—from a drunken sailor to a preacher of the Gospel. I remembered how He had given me a brand new car, absolutely free. I remembered how I'd been saved from a deliberate murder attempt. Every incident that came to my mind evoked more praise. I lifted my hands to heaven and worshipped in God's presence. "Oh, God, You've been so good to me!" I exclaimed. "I worship You! I praise You!"

Shortly after noon, the telephone rang.

16

"Brother Thom?"

"Yes."

"This is Brother Chambers. Would you like to have a steak with me today?" Walt Chambers was a friend I had met in Ohio at a tent revival.

"Well," I said, half-drooling at the thought of a juicy steak, "I'd love to; I appreciate your invitation. But, you see, I'm taking today off to praise the Lord."

"You're *what?*" he said with a slight chuckle.

"This is my day to offer God the sacrifice of praise," I explained. "I'm taking the day off to praise the Lord for something I need. I've made a covenant with God to praise Him all day today, and the need I have will be supplied, because God lives in the praises of His people."

"I never *heard* such a thing!" he exclaimed. "Anyway, that means we won't be able to get together today, doesn't it? Let's see—how about tomorrow?"

"Okay, Walt," I replied. "That's very kind of you. If you can pick me up tomorrow at midday, I'll be happy to have lunch with you."

"I'll be there," he assured me. Thanking him again and hanging up the phone, I went back to praising God for my $2,000.

The next day, Brother Chambers picked me up and we drove to a restaurant in downtown Zanesville. As we sat down to lunch, he said to me, "Brother Thom, I've just sold a nice piece of property, and now I owe the Lord some tithe money. *Would it be all right if I just gave you a check for $2,000?*"

I praised the Lord right out loud! "Brother Chambers," I said, struggling to keep my voice down, "this *has* to be a miracle! Do you know that this is the *exact amount* that I was praising God for yesterday?"

We then praised the Lord together, and he took out his checkbook and began to write.

When I got back to my motel room, I looked at that check again and again with tear-filled eyes. Once again, God had proved His faithfulness to me. Had He not said, "My God shall supply all your need according to his riches in glory . . ." (Philippians 4:19)? It was on the basis of *that promise* that I had praised God in advance the day before. I hadn't had any of the money at that point, but *I had God's Word*. I knew by experience that God *always* keeps His promises. If God said He'd supply my needs, then it was as good as done. So I had praised Him in faith. And now, here was the check in my hand. It wasn't any surprise though; it was just what I expected.

"Lord," I said, as I went to bed that night, "living by faith in You is the best way of all!" Adjusting my pillow to a more comfortable angle, I settled down for the night and began to recall how God had taught me to walk by faith. My mind went back to my boyhood days in South Africa where it had all begun in such an unlikely way. . . .

The Methodist Orphanage was located in a rural suburb called Rondebosch, about eight miles out of the busy city of Cape Town. The five red brick buildings housed about 180 strictly disciplined children. There were three girls' houses and two boys' houses. Even on sunny days, those old two-story buildings seemed drab and depressing—their black

18

roofs and gray dormers peering down at us like guards atop a prison wall.

It was in 1925 that my widowed mother took my sister and me to the orphanage; I was ten. Ma assured us that we would have good times with all the other children, and that the people in charge would give us plenty of love.

"You know, your father always believed in this place," Ma said to us. "Every year he gave $700 to the support of this home, and I'm sure he'd be glad to know that two of his children are being loved and trained by Christian people."

But I didn't understand the kind of love they had there. I guess they meant well, but the discipline was so rigid that it was hard to feel any love. I spent four long years in that place, and the longer I stayed, the more I hated it. I hated getting up at six o'clock on cold, foggy mornings and being forced to scrub the concrete floors with nothing more on than a thin shirt, short pants, and no shoes or socks.

"Dear God," I would sob as I knelt on the cold cement, wielding that scrub brush, "why did you let Daddy die? Why do I have to live here in this awful place? I want to go back home!"

But God never seemed to pay any attention to me. So week by week and month by month, I kept getting up on damp, shivery mornings and scrubbing those concrete floors. Soon I began to have a bad cough and shortness of breath. I didn't know it then, but the repeated exposure to those cold mornings was causing me to develop a serious asthmatic condition.

One morning when I was sure no one was looking, I slammed the wet scrub brush down and said,

"I hate this place! I hate it, I hate it, I HATE IT!"

"Oh, you do, do you?" a voice said behind me.

I looked up, shocked and ashamed that anyone had heard me. It was Sister Emily Dunn, the matron in charge!

"Come along with me, Robert," she said sternly. "You must learn to do what you are told without complaining. Haven't you read in the Bible that when people complain, it displeases the Lord?" And she took me up to her office, gave me a good thrashing in the name of the Lord, and sent me back down to finish my job.

After the early morning work was done, all of us were required to strip and take baths in ice cold water. I remember one particularly cold morning when one of the boys said, "Hey, you guys, there's ice in this water!" We all peered into the old-fashioned tub, and sure enough, a thin layer of ice covered the water.

"I'm not getting in there!" one boy shouted.

"Me neither!" another said.

"But if they don't hear water splashing, they'll know we're not taking our baths!" another boy cautioned.

"Then break the ice, and swish the water around a little!" another kid suggested. That sounded like a good idea to the rest of us; so, one by one, we all stuck a toe into the tub and kicked the water about three times to make it sound like we were bathing.

But what we didn't know was that Sister Emily Dunn was watching everything through a hole in the ceiling! After we'd gotten dressed, there she was waiting for us! She marched us all off to her office and got out her four-foot quince stick. "Shame on all of you!" she said. "Don't you know the Bible says, 'Be sure your sin will find you out'? If it is too cold to take a bath today, then perhaps *this* will warm you up, eh?" And, one by one, she bent our palms down tightly and delivered sharp, stinging blows to our hands with that dreaded stick.

"Now get down to the dining room and eat your breakfast!" she snapped. "And don't ever again let me catch you not taking a bath!"

"Yes, ma'am!" we sang in chorus, and quickly trooped down to join the others. With every step, I was saying under my breath, "I hate this place! God, how I hate it! Them and their religion! I hate it all!"

In the dining room, we stood like soldiers and repeated the same prayer we always used before every meal: "May the Lord make us truly grateful for this that we are about to receive. Amen." I even hated that prayer. Same old prayer, three times a day, day in and day out. To me, it was disgusting.

After a breakfast of porridge, thick slices of bread, and cups of cocoa, we had to wash the dishes. My assignment was to scrub the big pots and pans. I usually finished the job just in time to dash off to class.

We had school at the orphanage, which was one of the few things I enjoyed about that place. In South Africa the education is quite advanced, due to the considerable amount of preschool training which is required. Because of this, I was expecting to graduate at age fourteen. Not wanting to stay at that orphanage a day longer than necessary, I worked hard at my studies so I could graduate on time. All four years I was at the top of my class.

After the morning classes, we'd be back in the dining room saying that same old prayer: "May the

Lord make us truly grateful for this that we are about to receive. Amen." I doubt if even one of us gave any thought to what we were saying. It was a strictly mechanical routine we went through, and anybody who wanted to eat had better say those "passwords."

After lunch, there were more pots and pans to scrub before we went off to afternoon classes. School was out at three-thirty, and then for an hour we'd scrub and wax floors some more. By the time we were finished, those floors shone so brightly you could actually see the reflection of your face in them.

We were permitted an hour of play before supper. If it hadn't been for that hour, all of us might have gone crazy. But even then we were carefully watched, lest we become too raucous. Still, it was better than nothing, and we were grateful for a little relief from the grinding discipline of the day.

At five-thirty, we assembled in the dining room for supper. Again there was the dull repetition of childish voices in hollow unison, grinding out that prayer: "May the Lord make us truly grateful. . . ."

Sometimes as I sat at the table, my mind would go back to those happy days in Oudtshoorn, three hundred miles away. We were rich then. I remembered it all so clearly: the arching shade trees on our front lawn; the twelve-bedroom stone house on High Street, standing like a stately plantation mansion; my mother riding off to do her shopping in a handsome cab drawn by six white horses, with gorgeous white ostrich plumes in their harnesses; the servants who waxed the floors, weeded the gardens, washed and ironed our clothes, and waited on us at the table; my seven brothers and sisters, and the faithful servants who watched over us and played games with us under the trees.

My father, Alexander Thom, was a big, blond Scotchman, six feet four inches tall, and one of the prominent business men of Oudtshoorn. Oudtshoorn was the ostrich capital of the world, and owed its success to the fashionable women all over the world who were wearing those elegant ostrich plumes on their hats. My father was a jeweler, but when he saw what was happening in the ostrich feather market, he decided it would be a good side investment to help finance some ostrich farmers in the area who wanted to increase the size of their flocks. For a time, it seemed that he had made a wise investment, and the profits rolled in. But one day in 1922, my father came home with bad news.

"Maria," I heard him say to my dark-haired Irish mother, "the feather business is going downhill."

"Oh?" she replied with some surprise. "Does that mean we're in trouble?"

"Well, it's bound to be a bad thing for the ostrich farmers. And can you imagine what will happen to us if the farmers are forced out of business? After all that money I loaned them. . . ."

Ma stood in deep thought for a moment, seemingly not knowing what to say. But only for a moment. "Maybe it's not as bad as it seems," she said, trying to comfort my father. "Every business has its bad days."

"A bad *day* we can tolerate," he replied, "but when it goes into *weeks*, you know things aren't good."

When the big smash finally came a few months later, it hit us hard. Farmers all around the area

23

owed us money and were unable to pay. My father still had the jewelry shop, of course, but I can remember that we had some desperate times of prayer together when we gathered for our customary family devotions. I remember well how embarrassed the young fellows were who came courting my sisters during those days, when my father made them sit through our prayer sessions before going anywhere!

Poor rich people! Somehow, God saw us through those difficult days without too much loss, except a little damaged pride. Ma testified that God had heard our prayers, and I believed He had!

Every now and then, in those prayer times, Dad would get to talking about death. "You know what I'd like?" he'd say. "When I die, I'd like to go to be with the Lord on the same day that my Savior died: Good Friday. Wouldn't that be a fine day to go?"

"Oh, Dad," Ma would reply sadly, "must you always be talking about dying?"

"Well, we've all got to die *someday*," Daddy would reply. "And Good Friday would suit me just fine."

"Well, I don't see what difference it should make about the *day* you die," Ma would say.

"Maybe not," Daddy answered, "but the Lord has granted smaller requests than *that*, hasn't He?"

My father was a peculiar man. He was a Presbyterian of sorts with great interest in the Bible and prayer; yet I can't remember ever seeing him in church. But he was respected by all the townspeople as a man of deep devotion, and he was greatly loved, especially by the underprivileged people of the Cape.

I remember the day he died. I was only ten years

old. Daddy had been suffering from a respiratory problem, and his breathing had been becoming increasingly difficult. One day, when he still hadn't gotten up by noon, I went into his bedroom to see why he was sleeping so long. There he was, breathing hard. For a moment, I watched him holding his sides, battling for every breath. Then I darted back out to get my mother.

"You'd better check on Daddy," I called out. "He's not looking very well."

She could tell by the tone of my voice that I was badly frightened. She hurried into his bedroom and was obviously shocked to find him laboring so to get his breath. He was only fifty-two years of age, and it never dawned on her that he could be *that* sick. She tried to help him, but nothing she could do made it any easier for him. He continued to get worse, and at exactly 3:00 p.m., completely unexpected, he passed away. In our shock, it never occurred to us until a while later that it was *Good Friday*. . . .

When we laid my father away, both sides of the streets were lined with poor people for the entire three miles to the cemetery—a unique thing in South Africa. Those people loved my father.

It was shortly after Daddy's funeral that Ma decided to send my sister and me to the Methodist Orphanage three hundred miles away. It was an awful decision for her to make. So suddenly, her world had fallen to pieces! Never expecting to die so young, Dad hadn't made out his will. Ma was left with nothing. He was about $50,000 in debt, and Ma didn't think she had enough of a business head to handle all the details of the jewelry business.

"I can't *do* it," she sobbed. "Alexander always

handled the business, and it's just too much responsibility for me."

The local magistrate offered to help her, but that $50,000 seemed like an immovable mountain to her. So she decided to walk out and let the property go up for sale. The jewelry shop, the big stone house, the furniture, and our horses—she brokenheartedly walked out on it all, and went to Capetown. . . .

The screeching of chairs being pushed away from the tables in our orphanage dining room brought me back to reality with a jolt. I had been so completely immersed in the memories of Oudtshoorn that I had hardly been aware of the passing of time. Quickly I scooped up the last two or three bites of potatoes from my plate, put them all into my mouth at once, and jumped up from the table to catch up with the other boys who were heading for kitchen duty.

After the kitchen was in proper order, we were then sent off to our rooms to study until bedtime. At eight o'clock we mumbled through a memorized prayer, fell into bed tired and exhausted—and the lights were turned out.

Ma had rented a little house out in Maitland only about four miles from the orphanage. But much to our sorrow, she was permitted to come and see my sister and me only four times a year. It was usually on a Saturday afternoon. At first, I looked forward to her visits with much eagerness—but after a year or two, our love wasn't the same any more. We lived in our little world and she lived in hers. Sometimes it was hard to know what to talk about when she came, and we sat there awkwardly, like strangers straining to get a conversation started.

The only other diversion from the cheerless routine of the Methodist Orphanage was the three-week holiday at Christmastime. As the time drew near each year, we could scarcely restrain the wiggles and giggles that seemed to come so naturally when we thought about getting out of our "prison" for a few weeks. But we knew we must keep our gaiety to ourselves. It would have been very bad had Sister Emily Dunn known how eager we were to leave!

But somehow, those vacations were always a little disappointing to me. It was hard to forget all the rigorous disciplines of the orphanage. Sister Emily Dunn seemed to watch over me like a silent specter. Her iron-clad religion had me walled in, like the fortifications that walled in Jericho.

Ma's new home was a disappointment too. I missed our palatial stone house on High Street, the sprawling lawn where we used to play, and my own pleasant bedroom. The change must have been as difficult for her as it was for us, though she never said a word about it. She made her living by caring for elderly people, doing housework and other odd jobs. Remembering the servants we had had in Oudtshoorn, I wondered how she could be so cheerful and outgoing.

"That's a bad cough you have there, Bobbie," she would say. "Come here and take a dose of my cough medicine."

I took dose after dose of her medicine, but it didn't help much.

"How on earth did you ever catch such a cold?" she asked with great concern. "Haven't you been wearing your coat when you go out to play?"

"Yes'm, I always wear my coat," I said. "It's

really nothing to worry about—just a little cough. I'll probably be over it in a few days." I didn't want to tell her about scrubbing those cement floors and about how cold it was early in the morning.

By the time the third week of vacation rolled around, a spirit of melancholy began to grip me as I began to realize that we would soon be going back to the orphanage for another year. I wanted to tell Ma how much I hated it, but I could never bring myself to do so. Probably she knew anyway.

I fought tears all the way back to the orphanage. Before she left me, Ma laid her hand on my head and said, "I'll be praying for you, Bobbie. You know how your father and me have always wanted a minister in the family. And you're going to be a right *good* one!" And away she went.

"Minister! Not *me!*" I was so sick of religion I could die! "*Dear* Sister Emily Dunn, and her stinking prayers! Prayers—every morning—every night—every mealtime! Same old religious yak-ity-yak over and over! I'm so sick of it all I could throw up!

"Dear God," I prayed that night, "there *must* be more to the Christian life than I'm seeing *here.*" After some thought, I surprised myself by adding, "You know, I really *would* like to be a minister as Daddy and Ma said—but not if I have to be like these people here!"

I lay down on my cot, feeling a little guilty for thinking such evil thoughts. After all, the orphanage people *were* feeding and clothing us and giving us an education. It wasn't that I didn't appreciate this. But something was missing—an indefinable something that I desperately needed. I lay there in the dark with tears streaming down my face, trying to figure out what was wrong.

A few evenings later, all one hundred and eighty of us gathered in the orphanage church to hear a student minister preach. I don't remember his name but I'll never forget what he said.

"God really *loves* you," he declared earnestly. "You kids *mean* something to God. You're very special to Him!"

I drank in every word. So did the others. His words fell like drops of rain on a wilted garden. "Love!" We hadn't heard anything about that for a long time!

"Listen to me," the young preacher went on. "God loved you so much that He sent His only begotten Son to *die* for you! Jesus gave His life and shed His blood to pay the penalty for your sins. And you can know Jesus and you can experience His love if you'll just ask Him into your life!"

When I got back to the dormitory that night, I couldn't get to sleep. I tossed restlessly for several hours and kept thinking about God and wondering if He really *did* love me.

"God," I prayed under my breath, "if You really *are* God, and if You truly are interested in me, then appear to me tonight and let me be conscious of Your presence next to my bed."

I had no sooner prayed that prayer than I heard the church clock striking midnight. I had heard those doleful chimes many times before, but this time they sounded like the harps of angels. Immediately I became aware of God's presence. His glory swept over me like waves and waves of liquid electricity. It was almost as if I could feel Him bending over me as He whispered, "I love you."

For a long time, I cried and cried. I just couldn't get over it. God loved ME!

CHAPTER TWO

ONE PEPPERMINT BRANDY

I graduated from orphanage school in 1929 at the age of fourteen. Sister Emily Dunn treated me very nicely that day, although I wondered if her happiness was due to the fact that she was finally getting rid of me. All graduates received a brand-new outfit of clothing, two pairs of shoes and a pair of boots. We were then turned out into the world to shift for ourselves. But I went home with high hopes of continuing my education.

However, as Ma took me home to her three-bedroom brick home in Maitland, she made it clear that I would have to find a job and help with our living expenses. Alec, Leslie and Myra, my older brothers and sister who were still at home, were all working to help, and I would have to do the same.

A few days later, my brother helped me get a job as a helper in the accounting department of the Otis Elevator Company for the ridiculously low salary of four dollars and thirty-five cents a week.

"Ma," I said hesitatingly, "is it all right if I give you four dollars and keep the thirty-five cents?" Four dollars wasn't much, I knew, but I hoped it would at least help pay our rent—which was eight dollars and forty cents a month.

"Bobbie," she said sadly, "you know I wouldn't accept it from you if things weren't so bad. Maybe

30

things will get better later on. But until then, we'll just have to keep pooling what money we have to make ends meet."

But I knew it would never be any different unless I could get some additional training in order to qualify myself for a better job. So I talked it over with Ma, and finally she agreed to let me attend night school, though it was a great burden on her.

As I came and went, I soon became aware that all was not well in our home. There was a coldness in the air that bothered me. We rarely talked to one another, except when we were fighting. Anyway, Alec and Leslie hardly knew me, and since they were in their twenties and I was only fourteen, there seemed to be little to say.

Then there was the problem of church. Since my encounter with God at the orphanage, my life had been a good deal different. So when I came to live in Maitland, I made up my mind I would attend the Methodist Church there. But I could see I was in for a bad time on the very first Sunday morning. Alec and Leslie had been out late the night before, and were trying to get some sleep. I was trying to get ready for church as quietly as possible, but the splashing of water and pacing back and forth between my dresser and the mirror disturbed Alec.

"Hey, kid, watcha doin' in there?" he called from his bedroom.

"Gettin' ready," I replied timidly.

"Gettin' ready for *what?*"

"To go somewhere."

By that time, Leslie was awake too. They both rolled out of bed and shuffled over to the door of my bedroom, only half awake.

"Ahhh, *I* get it!" Alec sneered groggily, gazing at

31

my white shirt and tie. "You're going to *church*, aren't you?"

"Yes," I replied, with downcast eyes. "What's it to *you?*"

"Don't you know nobody goes to church in this family?" Leslie snorted.

"Maybe they ought to, though," I replied, trying to gather up courage.

"Don't get smart with us, kid," Alec threatened. "We don't need none of your religion around here!"

"That's right," Leslie added. "We don't believe in that stuff."

"Alec! Leslie!" I heard my mother calling from her bedroom. "Let him alone!"

They went back to their room, but from that time on, they avoided me like I had leprosy. Myra talked to me once in a while, and mother tried to be good to me, but for the most part, it was a lonely life.

Almost every Saturday night, Alec and Leslie had their friends over for a card game. One particular Saturday night after I had gone to bed, I heard my mother arguing with them about something.

"You know your father wouldn't put up with this gambling, and I'm not going to either!" Ma was saying.

"It's *my* money, isn't it?" Alec sassed.

"But you *said* you would help with the expenses of the house," she complained loudly. "And here you are gambling everything away!"

"You mean to tell us we can't have a little fun with our friends once in a while?" Leslie demanded. "What the h―― are you trying to do anyway?"

32

"I'm trying to keep a home together!" Ma screamed. "And what do *you* care?"

"Don't scream at me, old lady!" Alec bit out. "I don't have to take your lip!"

"Get out!" Ma snapped.

"Make us!" Leslie countered.

And then I heard a general scuffling and shouting and thumping of upsetting chairs. I jumped out of bed in time to see Ma shoving and pushing the whole gang of them out the door. They were tossing cards in the air and cursing a blue streak. It was almost funny to see my little mother handling them so efficiently. I tiptoed back to bed quickly before she saw me. Before I finally went back to sleep, I vowed that I would never cause my mother the heartache that Alec and Leslie were causing her. But little did I know. . . .

By the time I was seventeen, I had quit attending church and was a very bored person. So weary was I of life at home that I almost wished I were back in the orphanage.

It was 1933. One evening, not being able to put up with my boredom any longer, I decided to go over to a dance at All Saints Hall, the Episcopalian church hall, to see if anything exciting was going on.

There was! The prettiest girl I had ever seen was out on that dance floor. She was a sparkling little blond with smiling Irish eyes. She was as dainty as a butterfly, and as graceful—just a mite of a thing— and the longer I watched her, the more I liked her.

I would have given anything to meet her, but I was always embarrassed to be around girls, so I just stood there with my hands in my pockets, pretending I wasn't interested in dancing. But she noticed me, and between dances she came over to the corner where I was standing.

"Hi!" she said, smiling. "I'm Joyce O'Connor. What's *your* name?"

"Oh," I said, clearing my throat in surprise, "my name's Robert—Robert Thom."

"Do you like to dance?" she asked.

"Well—er—I don't know if—I mean, I—"

"You mean you don't know how to dance?"

"Well, not very well. . . ."

"That's okay, I'll teach you! C'mon!"

And with that she took me by the hand and pulled me out on that dance floor, and began to show me some steps. At first I felt so clumsy I could have died. But after a while, I got the hang of it and actually began to enjoy it.

After two or three dances, she smiled at me and said, "Thanks, Robert. We'll try that again sometime!" And with that, she was off and dancing with another boy.

I determined that I would get her attention again before the evening was over. Obviously, my dancing skill wouldn't dazzle her, so I decided to play the big he-man role. Between dances, I sauntered up to her and said, "Hey, Joyce, how 'bout going with me over to the Lord Milner Hotel for a drink?"

"Good idea," she said. "A coke would hit the spot right now."

So we went over to the hotel lounge next door and sat down at a table. After Joyce ordered her coke, I decided to impress her by ordering something stronger for myself. "I'll have a peppermint brandy," I said to the waiter.

That was my first drink. But it wasn't to be my

last. Through time, I found closer friendship with Joyce, and we began to date more regularly. We loved dancing and going out. Every now and then, I'd have another drink—usually a beer—although Joyce never drank with me.

When Ma discovered that I was drinking occasionally, she decided it was time to have a little heart-to-heart talk with me.

"Bob," she said solemnly, "I'm not forbidding you to drink. You're old enough to make up your own mind about that. But be careful. Too much drink is a terrible thing. And if you should turn out to be a drunkard, you'd break my heart."

She knew there was no use forbidding me to drink. We had always had liquor at our parties in the house. She, being a "good Methodist church-goer," saw no wrong in that. In fact, almost all the church people I knew kept liquor in their homes.

Within a year, I was drinking more regularly. One Saturday night, I came home drunk. When Ma saw me, she started to cry.

"What did I tell you?" she said. "Didn't I warn you that too much drink would make a fool out of you?"

"Get out of my way—I'm sick!" I said, staggering past her toward the bathroom.

"You *ought* to be sick," she blurted out. "I hope you get so sick you'll never take another drink again!"

I brought it all up in the bathroom, and vowed I'd quit. I rolled into bed, put my arm around my pillow, and mumbled, "Joycie, I love you. . . ." The next day I had a bad headache all day long.

About three weeks later, however, I came home drunk again. Ma hit the ceiling. "Bob, what's got into you?" she demanded angrily. "Don't you think I have enough trouble without your bringing this disgrace on me?"

"I'm not hurting anybody," I said. "I'm old enough to do what I please."

"Bob," she said sadly, "can't you see what you're doing to our home? Do you think God is pleased with the way you're acting?"

"Shut up!" I snapped. "God don't have anything to do with it." And I walked away from her to my bedroom.

"Well, I'm going to pray for you," she called from the living room. "Only the good Lord can help you!" Little did she know that she would have to pray for me for sixteen years!

In 1935, Joyce and I got married. I was only twenty years of age. At first, we were happy together and I even cut down on my drinking some. But little by little, I became more careless. One Saturday night, I didn't come in until two a.m. When I finally got home, I found Joyce waiting for me with red, swollen eyes.

"Bob," she said quietly, "I'm not mad at you—but I *am* a little disappointed."

"Now, Baby," I said, looking at her with glassy eyes and slobber running out of the corners of my mouth, "would I ever deliberately disappoint you?"

She just stared at me for a moment in disbelief. Then she buried her face in her arms and sobbed and sobbed.

The next morning, she made me promise to quit drinking. "I *will*, Honey," I declared. "If my drinking is making you unhappy, then that settles it. I've had my last drink."

I thought I meant it, but on my next payday, the old thirst came back. "Well," I thought to myself, "one small drink won't hurt." So before going home, I stopped off at a bar and ordered a glass of beer. From then on, I'm not quite sure what happened. All I know is that I got in around three a.m. Joyce was waiting for me again.

"Bob," she said, "what about that promise you made me?"

"*What* promise?" I laughed. "The only promise I ever made you was to love, honor and cherish you till beer do us part!" I was so drunk I didn't know what I was saying.

Things began to get worse after Drummond was born. More and more money was needed for milk, baby food and clothing. Though I had a good job by that time, still my drinking habit was taking a bigger and bigger bite out of my paycheck. Every Friday night, I was stopping off at the bar and drinking my money away—often getting so drunk that I would black out and fall off the bar stool.

Joyce was finding it more and more difficult to be patient with me. I was hardly ever at home, the bills were piling up, and I didn't care. The bottle was all that mattered.

One Wednesday evening, Joyce said to me, "Bob, the rent is two months past due. The landlord wants to know when you're going to pay."

Without lowering the newspaper I was reading, I said carelessly, "I'll pay it when I'm good and ready."

"Bob, you can't continue acting like this!" she warned. "The landlord will put us out if we don't pay."

"Put us out? Him and who else?" I sneered.

"Him and the magistrate, that's who!"

"Let 'em do it if they're big enough!"

About that time, Joyce could contain her anger no longer. She walked over to where I was sitting and ripped the newspaper away from my face. "You fool!" she shrieked. "All you think about is your liquor! Doesn't it mean *anything* to you that you've got a family? Can't you ever think of *anyone* but *yourself?*"

I jumped to my feet and slapped her across the face. "I'll teach you to talk to your husband that way!" I snorted. Then, turning on my heel, I stalked out of the house, calling back as I left, "Tell that d—— landlord he'll get his money on Saturday!" And I slammed the door and went down to the bar.

I did a little deep thinking over a glass of beer that night. Things had changed a lot since Joyce and I first got married. I could see how my foolishness had embittered her. Sweet little Joycie! I remembered how beautiful she'd been on that night when I first met her. I remembered the sweet scent of the perfume she wore. I drained my glass dry and just sat there and reminisced for a while. "Well," I said finally, "I've got to stop *sometime*— and this might as well be it.

"One last beer!" I called out to the bartender. He grinned and set a new glass in front of me. I drank it down, and staggered home.

When Friday evening came, I had already made up my mind that the first thing to come out of my pay would be the rent. "Can't let that rent go any longer," I mumbled to myself. "It's been too long already."

My determination was strong until I walked past

the bar. As soon as the aroma of beer reached my nostrils, I knew it wasn't going to be easy. By the time I was a block past the bar, though, I figured I had the battle licked.

But the farther I walked, the more I thought about how good a cold glass of beer would taste. I could see the froth trickling down the sides of the glass. I could feel the cold rivulets of golden beer running down my parched throat. I could feel the tingling sensation in my mouth. My imagination went wild. I saw myself drinking one glass of beer after another. The more I drank, the more I wanted. One after another. Faster and faster and faster.

"My God!" I screamed. "I can't stand it!" And I turned and *ran* back to the bar and ordered *two* beers. Before I left the bar that evening, I blacked out twice. Finally, the bartender said, "Tommy, you'd better go home. It's almost three o'clock."

Joyce was waiting for me when I stumbled into the house.

"You liar!" she screamed. "I might have known better than to believe *you!* You and your empty promises about paying the rent!"

I clenched my fists and glared at her for a moment, weaving to and fro. "Woman," I said through gritted teeth, "nobody talks to me like that and gets away with it!"

"Go ahead and hit me, you stupid drunk!" she sneered, raising her fists and poking at me. "I can play that game too!"

Her eyes were flashing with anger. Her knuckles were white. I reached out and gave her a shove, sending her sprawling back into a corner. "You dumb chicken!" I snorted. "I ought to blacken both your eyes!" By that time baby Drummond was awake and screaming.

Quick as a flash, she was on her feet. "You low-down bum!" she spat out. "I always knew you were no good! I can't stand any more of your beer guzzling and carousing around! I've had all I can take!" She drew back her fists and connected on my jaw with a crack. Then another. And another. I fell to the floor.

For a moment, I lay there in silence. Then, without saying a word, I gathered myself up and shuffled back to the bedroom. I felt nauseated. I tried to get ready for bed, but I was getting sicker by the minute. I couldn't hold it any longer; I vomited all over the bedspread. When it was all over, I jerked the bedspread off the bed, rolled it up into a ball, threw it into a corner, and plopped into bed in a drunken stupor. Before I fell asleep, I promised myself I'd never touch another drop of liquor.

But the next morning at six, I pulled a bottle of wine out from under the bed and drained it all before I got up.

CHAPTER THREE

A DRUNK IN THE HOLY LAND

Somehow we managed to keep our home together until the war broke out in 1940. By that time, Lionel had been born, and Joyce was expecting our third child. How we survived during those pre-war years I'll never understand. My liquor account was more than my grocery account. But we never starved. Some of Joyce's friends, knowing about my drinking problem, would bring in groceries and clothing to keep us going.

As soon as I learned about the war, I made up my mind I would join the Army. I knew I couldn't support my liquor habit and my family at the same time. I was sick of all the bills and burdens of family life, and this seemed like a good avenue of escape.

When I informed Joyce of my decision, I thought I detected a note of relief in her voice. Probably she was glad to get rid of me.

Two months after I enlisted in the South African Army, our third little boy was born. Joyce named him Roy. I went home to see her, but I was drunk most of the time I was on leave, so the visit meant little to either of us.

After basic training, our unit was shipped up north to the deserts of Egypt. Some of the guys were real concerned about getting shot up. But not me. My main worry was how I was going to get enough liquor up there in the desert.

My worries were not unfounded. When we first got into the desert, there were no facilities of any kind—no mess hall, no officers' quarters, no place to buy liquor. There were 16,000 of us in our unit, and it was our job to set up a camp at El Kantara. When they saw the situation, a lot of the other guys started complaining about not having any liquor.

Finally, one of them said, "There's only one man that can find us liquor."

"Thom!" they all shouted.

"Right! Thom's our man!"

So that night, they marched me out into the desert. "You'll find liquor, won't you, Tommy?"

"I'll do my d——dest," I said.

For a moment, I stood there trying to figure out what to do. Suddenly I said to the others, "See that light off in the distance there? Let's go that way!"

When we got there, we discovered that the light had been coming from a Canadian signal outpost. I did some nosing around while the other men engaged the officer in conversation. Pretty soon, I discovered cases and cases of Canadian beer buried in a dugout under the officer's bed!

"Hey, you guys!" I shouted. "Look what I found! Beer!"

"Yahooo!" they shouted, and scrambled in to see the treasure I'd found. We shoved the bed aside and began to help ourselves, while the Canadian stood there helplessly, watching us guzzle his beer!

"What'd I tell you?" one of our fellows said. "If anybody can find liquor, Tommy can. He's got a nose for it!"

It was true. I must have had a demon that led me, because I could find liquor anywhere.

I wrote to Joyce now and then, but there wasn't much heart in it. I knew she was better off without me around, and it hurt me to think about it, but that's the way it was. I had instructed the Army paymaster to send her half of my pay. I knew she needed more than that, but I had "expenses" too, so she would have to be satisfied with what I could send.

One night, after all of us had retired to our tents, I was lying there thinking about what a mess I'd made of my life. When I finally drifted off to sleep, I saw a procession of people parading before me in a dream. Sister Emily Dunn was first, shaking her finger at me and saying, "Shame on you! Don't you know the Bible says, 'Be sure your sin will find you out'?" Then I saw the beautiful face of my mother saying, "Bobbie, you know how your father and I have always wanted a minister in the family." Then there was that student minister saying, "God really *loves* you!" Then I saw the tearful face of Joyce saying, "Bob, what about that promise you made me?"

I woke up in a cold sweat, my heart pounding. "God," I said in the dark, "I don't know what's the matter with me. I guess You and me just don't have anything in common anymore. . . ." I rolled over and tried to get back to sleep; but I couldn't get those crazy thoughts out of my mind, so I got up and found a bottle of beer I had hidden away, and comforted myself with that until I got sleepy.

The next morning, I noticed Corporal Williams reading his New Testament. This guy really bothered me. Every morning I saw him sitting over there on his bunk reading that Bible.

"Now look at that sweet little Methodist!" I yelled loudly enough for everybody to hear. "He's having himself a little Sunday school!"

All the other guys chimed in with hee-haws and foot-stomping. But Williams read on. He was accustomed to my unmerciful taunting. Inwardly, I admired his quiet joy and good-natured smile. It made me wonder what his secret was.

A few weeks later, I had a ten-day leave coming to me. I decided I would hitchhike over to the Holy Land and do a little sight-seeing. Imagine! A drunk like me—going to the Holy Land! It was a dumb idea, I thought, but it wouldn't be more than a ten or twelve hour trip, and I was interested in seeing some of the places we'd studied about in the orphanage.

I got a fellow by the name of George Bancroft to go along with me. George was a Roman Catholic, and I figured he'd be interested in seeing some of the "holy sights" too.

It wasn't usually very difficult for soldiers to hitchhike; in a short time, a Polish fellow stopped and picked us up. George hopped into the back seat, while I took the front seat with the driver.

"We're going over to Jerusalem," I said to the driver. "You going that far?"

"Very good, okay," he said, flashing me a big smile.

"Good! My name's Thom, and this here is my buddy, Bancroft," I said, trying to get some conversation started.

"Very good, okay," he replied.

44

"We've got a ten-day leave, so Bancroft and I figured it would be a nice way to spend our vacation, looking over the holy places in Jerusalem. We plan to go down to Bethlehem and have a look around there too. It ought to be a nice trip, don't you think?"

"Very good, okay," he nodded approvingly.

I looked back at Bancroft and winked. "Watch this," I said behind the back of my hand. Clearing my throat, I looked at the driver and said, "Well, what do you think of this awful war?"

"Very good, okay!" he replied.

Bancroft and I exploded in laughter. The driver looked at us and figured he'd cracked a good one, so he laughed too. It took us ten hours' continuous driving to get to Jerusalem. Giving up on making conversation with a Pole who couldn't say anything in English but "Very good, okay," we smoked one cigarette after another. When Bancroft and I got out, we thanked our friend for his kindness. "Very good, okay!" he said as he waved and drove away.

"Bancroft," I said, "if you ever mention the words 'very good, okay' to me again, you and I are finished!"

We picked up our bags and went to hunt up a place where we could have a drink. We finally located the Vienna Bar and went in and had a vodka. I could have had lots more, but I didn't want to get drunk in the Holy City, so I limited myself to one.

Around noon, we went over to the Garden of Gethsemane, the place where Jesus had often prayed. Not many tourists were there that day, although it was a perfect day for sight-seeing. I'll never forget the strange feeling I had as we stepped into the shade of that Garden.

"I'm going into the church," Bancroft said. "Want to come along?"

"No, thanks," I replied. "I think I'll just stay out here." So Bancroft went on into the Franciscan church, and I was left alone.

I decided to stroll along the pathways which looped around the ancient olive trees. At times I stopped and gazed at those strange old trees. The trunks were large and gnarled, like sturdy old soldiers that refused to die. As old as they were, still they supported an impressive growth of branches which shaded the pathways. The golden sun was filtering down through the grayish-green foliage. There wasn't a sound except for the faint rustling of leaves.

As I stood there in the quietness of that place, I sensed the Presence of a Man near me. For a moment, it stunned me. I wanted to look at Him, but I was afraid He would be withheld from my gaze. But I knew Who it was. It was the same divine Presence I had felt years before in the orphanage. The power that radiated from Him was all so familiar. He didn't say a word—but I was deeply convicted by His Presence. My whole body trembled and my eyes filled with tears. . . .

When Bancroft finally came out of the church, I was a little embarrassed at the wetness of my eyes, and hoped he wouldn't notice. Thankfully he didn't.

We had stayed in the Garden a little longer than we'd planned, so we had to hurry on over to Calvary and the Garden Tomb. The same divine Presence I had felt under the olive trees continued to linger with me, in spite of our haste.

Later in the afternoon we hitchhiked the five

46

miles to Bethlehem on an Army truck. Both of us wanted to see the Church of the Nativity, which supposedly marks the place where Jesus was born.

Our guide told us this was the oldest church in Christendom. Except for the three belfries, it looked more like a complex of fortified military structures. Its gray stone walls were tall and rugged, with very small windows. Quite a number of tourists were there that day. Before we were permitted to enter the church, however, we had to purchase a candle. They were selling them for ten cents apiece. Then our guide led us to a very small opening in the wall, not more than four feet high.

"This is the entrance to the church," he announced. "You will need to get down on your hands and knees to get in." He then dropped to all fours and crawled into the church, with Bancroft and me behind him.

Once in, I said to the guide, "This is strange. Why must you get on your hands and knees to enter this church?"

"Ah," he said, with a twinkle in his eye, "even the King of England must bow on his knees when he goes into the place where the King of Kings was born!"

"Yes," I said, "but what is the *real* explanation?"

"The Crusaders made it that way," he said. "You see, when the church was first built, the door was originally eighteen feet high. It was made that way so the warriors on horseback could enter with ease. But a doorway that large proved to be a real problem in defending the church against attackers; so finally they decided to reduce it to four feet, so they could defend the building more easily."

"And that's the *real* explanation?"

"Let us say that this is *one* explanation," he answered. "We Christians here in Bethlehem still believe that God had a hand in making the entrance of this church in such a way that every knee must bow."

"Maybe so," I replied skeptically as we walked on through the foyer.

Soon we entered an elegant, five-aisled basilica, colonnaded on both sides. Walking to the front of the basilica, we went through a doorway and down a flight of steps to the place of Jesus' birth. As we waited in line to kneel in front of the brass star on the floor which supposedly marks the exact spot, I noticed a man ahead of us who was in the uniform of the Royal Air Force. As he knelt to the right of the star with his candle, that big strapping corporal began to weep and pray like a little child. It was very quiet, and we could hear every word he prayed. "Thank You, Lord, that You came down to this manger to be born for me," he said. "Thank You, Lord, that You saved my soul!" And he knelt there and wept unashamedly.

Again, I felt that same Presence sweep over me. It was more than I could bear to see that big soldier weeping like that. I turned away, and began to walk out. Just as I was about to go back upstairs, a bearded, Greek Orthodox priest came up to me, laid his hands on my shoulder and prayed, "And may the soul of this pilgrim be saved in Jesus' name, that will be a shilling please, amen."

I paid the shilling with some amusement, and breathed a silent prayer that God would answer the old priest's petition. I felt sure God was trying to tell me something.

A few days later Bancroft and I got back to our

military camp in Egypt. It was about five o'clock in the afternoon, and the mess halls were just opening; a lot of the fellows were going in for drinks. I stood there for a few minutes, my eyes eagerly scanning the crowd for a certain man. Suddenly I spotted him.

"Chaplain, Sir!" I shouted. "Chaplain, I must speak to you!" He was on his way to get *his* drink too.

"Yes," he replied somewhat impatiently, "what is it?"

"Sir, I've just come back from Jerusalem, and I don't know what's the matter with me. I can't swear, I can't take a drink, I can't even smoke a cigarette! I need help! I must speak to you. I want to get saved!"

He surveyed me from head to foot for a moment, then said, "Sorry, Soldier, I'm too busy—maybe some other time." And he went on into the mess hall to have his drink.

I wanted to get mad. I wanted to cuss him out—but I couldn't. In fact, for the next two weeks, I couldn't take a drink or light a cigarette. I couldn't even go to a movie! All I could do was think about Jesus! I kept looking around for something to read that would tell me how to get saved. I finally found a modern translation of Paul's epistles. How I enjoyed reading that book! It was like a drink of cold water in the middle of a desert. Even though I didn't understand all that I read, I felt like I was on the right track.

My drinking buddies couldn't understand what had happened to me.

"Hey, Tommy," they would say, "*come on*, let's have a *drink!*"

49

"Thanks," I would say, "but I'm not drinking anymore!"

"Man, what's the matter with you?" they countered. "You always drank with us before. You bomb-happy or somethin'?"

"Maybe this d——— desert life is getting to him," another suggested.

"Yeah," another said, "and guess who's goin' off their rocker next? ME!"

"Wait a minute, you guys," I pleaded. "I can explain everything if you'll just give me a chance."

"Okay, you guys," one of them piped up. "Gather 'round and hear a crazy man explain why he's nuts!"

"Will you knock it off?" I said impatiently.

"Okay, man, okay! We're all ears."

"It all started when Bancroft and I went on that trip over to the Holy Land. . . ."

"Uh-oh, here it comes, you guys!" one of them interrupted. "What'd I tell you?" And he started yodeling *The Old Rugged Cross* in a high squeaky voice.

"Shut up, will you?" one of the others said.

"Yeah," the others chorused. "This we gotta hear!"

When I finished my story, they all laughed and hollered and pounded me on the back.

"Amen, brother!" one shouted. "You got the old-time religion!"

"Praise the Lord and pass the beer!"

"Hey, honey, how about a highball?"

"Halleluyer! This man is SAVED!"

"Yahoo!"

I was so mad I could have chewed up nails. I elbowed my way through the ring of laughing fellows around me and headed for the mess hall.

"I'll show those idiots," I muttered to myself. "I can put away more beer than *any* of 'em!"

But when I came to the mess hall door, I couldn't go in. I can't explain why; I just couldn't. . . .

CHAPTER FOUR

OF ALL THE CRAZY DEVELOPMENTS!

A few days later, we moved out of Egypt to the European theater of war in Italy. That was in 1943. We first landed in Taranto, and then crossed over into Naples. From there, we moved up behind the American and British forces into Rome, took over some factories and began producing supplies needed by the Allied Forces.

The whole time I was in Rome, I kept looking for God. Every time German bombers flew low over our barracks, I realized how easily my life could be snuffed out. At any time, day or night, the Germans could drop a payload on us, and we'd be blasted into eternity. So, on weekends, I began to search for God in many of Rome's largest churches. But it was discouraging business. No matter where I looked, God seemed very far away.

One day, in desperation, I went to the Vatican and prayed in St. Peter's Cathedral. "Surely I ought to be able to find God *here*," I thought. But nothing happened.

However, as I left the church, I was stopped by a young black-haired Italian woman with a baby on her hip.

"Hey, Soldier," she called, taking hold of my elbow, "you help poor war-widow, no?"

"Why certainly, ma'am," I replied. "What can I do for you?"

She leaned over closer and whispered in my ear, "You coma my house and sleep with me tonight? I sleep with you all night cheap!"

I drew back from her in disgust. "Look, lady, I got enough troubles," I said. "You oughta be ashamed of yourself!"

"I'ma sorry, Soldier. I got no other way maka mon! My baby, he'sa starve. Nobody care. My husband, he'sa dead. My family, they no help me."

"Well, what about the church?" I said. "They ought to be able to help you. What church do you belong to?"

"Church?" she replied. "I go *this* church!"

"St. Peter's?"

"Yeah."

"And you can't get any help from them?"

"No, Soldier. They no help trash like me."

"I'll be d——ed," I said. "If this is God, I don't want to know Him!" I gave her a few dollars and walked on down the street, very discouraged. "These d—— churches!" I said to myself. "They're all alike. They're just like those orphanage people: they *talk* about love, but they don't *have* any!"

The more I thought about it, the more disgusted I became. Here I'd been looking for God all over Rome, and what had it gotten me? Nothing but aching feet and disappointment. God? What did *He* care? I doubted if He even knew I existed.

In my discouragement, the old thirst for liquor began to return. What else was there to turn to? I couldn't see any further point in depriving myself of a good drink.

Liquor was scarce during the war years, but some of my friends had told me about a farmer who had a still on his farm just outside of Rome. So next Sunday afternoon, I hitchhiked out there to see if I could get a drink.

It was a hog farm. The air was heavy with the stench of manure and rotten garbage. Walking up to the barn where the farmer was working on an old wagon, I said, "Hey, I hear you got wine. Is that so?"

Without looking up from his work, he replied, "Yep. Red and white. You got money?"

"Sure," I replied. "How much to fill up a canteen?"

"Two dollars."

"What the h———! You're making money, aren't you?"

"Take it or leave it."

"I'll take it."

I gave him the money, and he led me around behind the barn and down into a little room.

"What'll it be, red or white?" he asked.

"Red."

After my canteen was filled, I went out and leaned over the dilapidated fence surrounding the pig pen, sipping the warm wine slowly and watching the hogs rooting around in the mud holes. One of the hogs came over to the fence and stuck his dripping, wet snout through the fence and sniffed at me. "Get out of here, you dumb pig!" I spat out, giving the fence a kick.

After I emptied the canteen, I got a fill-up of white wine "for the road," and hitchhiked back to Rome, drunker than I'd been for a long time. For the duration of my stay in Rome, I went out to the farm every Sunday.

Finally, in 1945, the war was over. Within six days, I was told that because of my excellent performance during the war, the Army had a very big job waiting for me in South Africa. So I was flown out of Italy on a VIP pass.

It was good to get back to Cape Town. I was given thirty days' leave before my new assignment, so I had some time to spend with Joyce and the children. Even though I now realized that I couldn't live without drinking, I dared to hope that perhaps things might be a little better between Joyce and me, after six years in the service.

They were. I couldn't understand it at first. Joyce seemed so relaxed and happy. The old tensions were gone. She didn't even seem to mind when I went out on that first Friday night and got drunk. But the mystery suddenly unraveled the night I caught her out in the kitchen with a bottle of beer in her hand.

"Joyce!" I yelled. "What the h—— are you doing?"

"Oh, didn't I tell you?" she replied, with a mischievous grin. "I've found a new pastime."

I stood there, paralyzed in unbelief, as she casually took two glasses from the cupboard, emptied the contents of the bottle into them, and then held one glass out to me. "Here," she said, "you look like you need a good drink."

I took the glass from her, hesitantly, and sat it down on the kitchen counter. "You mean to tell me *you're* drinking now?" I demanded.

"What's it look like, Soldier?" she replied as she sipped the froth from the top of her glass.

"Now wait a minute," I said, "no wife of mine is going to drink that slop!"

"Well, I don't see why not," she replied curtly. "If *you* can do it, so can *I!*"

I couldn't believe it. My wife! Drinking! Of all the crazy developments!

After a few days though, I grew accustomed to the idea, and we started having liquor brought to the house by the caseful. Now, in addition to going out with the boys on Friday or Saturday nights, I could drink any time I wanted to. And I did. I was drunk most of the time, and sometimes Joyce got drunk with me. I got so I couldn't stand more than a few hours between drinks. I had to have a drink the first thing in the morning. And at lunch. And dinner. I didn't care about eating. All I wanted was a good stiff drink.

At the end of the thirty days, I was given a job in the Demobilization Corps in Cape Town, getting the boys out of the service. They had a huge backlog of fellows who had been waiting for disability grants and allowances to go to college. In spite of my drinking problem, I plowed into that job and cleaned it up in three weeks.

My superior officers knew about my drinking problem and wanted to discharge me. In fact, I was drunk on the day the Army doctor examined me for discharge. After he completed his examination, he said to the officers, "If this man is discharged, his children will starve to death, because he'll never keep a job anywhere."

"Maybe so," one of the officers replied. "But six years in the Army is long enough."

I didn't agree. If my Army days were over, I decided I'd rather join the Navy. I knew I could get plenty of cheap liquor in the service, which was more than I could say for civilian life. So at 11:59 on July 1st, 1946, I was discharged from the Army, and two minutes later, I officially became a sailor in the South African Navy.

Because of my record of performance in the Army, I received six promotions on one order on my very first day in the Navy! Yet I couldn't even salute the Navy way! But because of my experience in accounting at Otis Elevator, they felt they had a job for me that I could handle: all the Navy war accounts had to be cleared up for conversion back to the peacetime Navy. In order to complete this job, I was assigned to H.M.S. Bon 1 Naval Base in Cape Town, which permitted me to live at home with my family.

During those days, it was the same old round again. Drinking myself crazy, living for the devil, no time for God, no time for church. Yet I claimed to be a good Methodist! The Navy doctor called me in one day and told me I'd consumed so much liquor that it had eaten away one of my kidneys. I found out later that he only told me this to frighten me so I'd quit drinking. But I couldn't stop. Not only was I drinking at home, but I was also going back to the bars more and more frequently. It looked like I was hooked for good.

CHAPTER FIVE

THAT "CRAZY" MRS. WEBSTER

In 1947, things began to happen in my family—most of them unknown to me at first. For one thing, Drummond, who was then eleven years old, had gone to a children's Easter service down at the beach and had been saved.

A few weeks later, Joyce decided to go to church one Sunday. She too responded to the simple message she heard, accepted Christ as her personal Savior, and gave up her drinking and life of sin. But none of this was known to me. Joyce was scared to tell me what had happened, and I was so drunk that Sunday that I didn't notice the change in her.

On Monday morning as I was leaving the house to go to my job down at the base, Joyce said to me, "Now come home decently tonight, and let's all have supper at six o'clock."

"Okay," I replied. "Six o'clock it is."

The amazing thing is that I actually *did* make it home by six that evening! Joyce had a mouth-watering supper prepared. I was hungry, so I sat down to the table with the rest of the family and dug in. Nobody said much, but somewhere about halfway through the meal, I looked across the table at Joyce. She was sitting there smiling at me!

For a few fleeting seconds, I saw her as she used to be—her smiling Irish eyes so full of love—her bubbly disposition radiating beauty and happiness. She almost looked that way again.

"What're *you* so happy about?" I spoke up.

"Oh, nothing much, I guess," she said hesitantly. "I feel good tonight."

"It's a good thing *somebody* does," I remarked, going back to my eating.

The next morning as I was leaving for work, she said, "Now you did fine last night; be home at six again tonight."

"I'll be here," I promised.

But I was beginning to get a little "dry," so I decided to stop off at the hotel bar for a few minutes before going home that evening. I ordered up a glass of lager beer and a double brandy, sipped the froth off the beer, and added half the brandy to it. After a couple of beers, I got into an argument with some of the other customers about who was the world's best boxer. By the time I got home, it was seven o'clock. I could see by the table that the rest of them had already eaten.

"I tried to keep your supper warm for you," Joyce said, taking some food out of the oven. "I'm afraid it won't be quite as good. . . ."

"That's okay," I said with a thick tongue, "I'm not too hungry anyway."

I tried to eat the delicious food she put in front of me, but it just wouldn't go down. Joyce tried to be cheerful that evening, but with me half drunk, there wasn't much point in it.

On Wednesday morning, she didn't say anything about my coming home on time. So again, I stopped off at the bar. I got home at eight-thirty.

"The food's all cold," she said sadly. "Do you want me to warm up something for you?"

"No," I replied, "I'm not hungry." That was the extent of our conversation for the rest of the evening.

Thursday night I came home at ten. The kids were already in bed. I was good and drunk, so I went straight to bed and left Joyce sitting alone in the living room.

Friday night I never came home. I drank one beer after another until seven o'clock. By that time I was so drunk I didn't know what I was doing. I knew I couldn't make it home, so I asked the bartender for a hotel room. Seeing how sick I was, he said, "There's a vacant room down at the end of the hall. Take that one."

I staggered out through a doorway and down the adjoining hall. I was faint and dizzy. That hall looked a mile long. I knew I couldn't make it, so I staggered past the black maid's quarters and went into the first open doorway I came to, threw myself down on the bed and blacked out.

When I woke up the next morning, my clothes were covered with chicken feathers! Those pesky feather-stuffed mattresses! Feathers were continually working through the covering and seams. But I was feeling too miserable to care about a few feathers. So I staggered over to the bar, ordered up another beer, paid for it and the room, and sat there for another fifteen minutes trying to wake up.

I got home Saturday morning just as Joyce was getting up. I had no idea what time it was. She just stared at the feathers all over me.

"Where have *you* been?"

"I blacked out," I said, not trying to explain

about the mattress. I went back to my bedroom, took off my uniform, laid it beside the bed, put my pajamas on and crawled under the covers. The soft pillow felt good. My head was splitting; but a few hours sleep would fix that, I thought. I sighed and closed my eyes.

Two minutes after I'd lain down, the alarm went off. It was time to get up and go to work! I rolled back the covers, took my pajamas off, picked the feathers off my uniform, put it on and went off to the shipyards.

At noon, I read in the newspaper that a black maid had been strangled to death in her room with a piece of wire sometime during Friday night—in the very hotel where I'd stayed. I tried to recall hearing any commotion or screaming. But my mind was a blank. All I could remember was staggering past a maid's room when I was on the verge of blacking out.

The article said that the authorities were looking for the murder suspect. Suddenly it dawned on me that the very fact that I was in the same building *automatically* made me a suspect! I dreaded the thought of perhaps being questioned by the police. If I had some sensible answers, it wouldn't be so bad —but as drunk as I was, I couldn't remember a thing.

"What're you worrying about?" I said to myself finally. "Just tell 'em you were sick and don't remember anything about it."

Relieved, I smiled to myself for a moment. But then another thought popped into my mind from somewhere. "Who's to say *you're* not the one who did it? You were blacked out, remember? You were irresponsible. You could have done almost anything in your sleep. And if they question you, how can you prove you *didn't* do it?"

I broke out in a sweat. I read and reread that article. I couldn't get it out of my mind all afternoon. "Am I a murderer?" I kept asking myself. Every time I heard footsteps behind me, I jumped, thinking it might be the police.

All the next week, I lived in fear. Every night, I would dream of devilish creatures pointing their bony fingers at me and crying, "Murderer! Murderer! Robert Thom's a murderer!" And then they would laugh in fiendish glee. Time and again, I'd wake up in a lather of sweat and beg God to take those cursed nightmares from me.

I tried to drown my fears in drink, but it was no good. Any minute, the police could be at my door. I spent every evening of that week at the bar.

On Saturday, I worked a half day and came home drunk as usual. Joyce and the baby were gone. She'd left a note for Drummond. I unfolded it and read the brief message:

I'm sorry—I can't stay here any more. Please take care of the other kids for me. There's roast beef and potatoes in the refrigerator. I love you.

Mommy

We had a quiet lunch that day, except that the kids kept asking where Mommy was.

"She had to go somewhere," I told them. "She'll be back." I couldn't eat anything for the lump in my throat.

After the kids were finished eating, I sent them

outside to play. I nervously sliced off a piece of roast beef, picked up a cold potato, and stood there at the window staring blankly at the big mountain behind our house.

I thought I would go out of my mind. It seemed that I didn't have a friend in the world. The police were probably looking for me. I was hopelessly hooked on liquor.

"D____!" I said to myself. "What's the use of living? I'm all washed up!" I stood there trying to figure out how I could end it all.

Just then someone knocked at the front door. When I opened the door, there stood a middle-aged woman in a tweed suit and close fitting hat. "How do you do?" she said. "Are you Robert Thom?"

"Yes, ma'am," I replied wearily. "What can I do for you?"

"My name is Gladys Webster," she said, brushing past me into the living room. We turned to face each other. "Mr. Thom," she said, "I've come to tell you about Jesus."

"Jesus!" I hooted. "Listen, you stupid woman, I don't need any Sunday school lessons! I got my church—I got my Bible—I'm a Methodist—and I don't need whatever it is you're peddling!"

"Where *is* your Bible?" she asked, still trying to smile bravely.

"It's in the bottom of my duffel bag where I put it when I left Rome in 1945! Now get the h____ out of my house before I break your skinny neck!"

She was scared. "All right, Mr. Thom," she said, backing out the door. "I'm sorry—I didn't mean to . . . ."

"Shut up!" I roared. "Just get off my property!"

"Yes, sir!" she replied as she bolted from the house.

"And don't ever come back!" I yelled.

I turned away from the doorway, glad to be rid of her. "These dumb fanatics!" I mumbled to myself. "I don't need any of their fool religion!"

But no sooner had I turned my back than I heard her coming up the walk again! She walked straight in, put her finger under my nose and began to pray in a language I'd never heard. (I had heard somewhere about people speaking in "tongues," and suspected that this was what she was doing.) I tried to back away from her and go to my bedroom, but suddenly an unseen Power took hold of me, and the next thing I knew, I was on my knees praying, my hands lifted toward the ceiling! I heard myself saying, "If there be a God in heaven, be merciful to me—a *sinner!*" and I began to weep profusely.

Immediately, she slapped her hand on my head and began rebuking every demon that was in me. "You devils, come out of him!" she shouted. "Satan, I *command* you to loose him and let him go—in the name of Jesus!"

Well! I had never had a treatment like *that* before! But as she prayed, I felt something strange happening to me—"a letting go" within—"a moving out" of strange forces. I began to laugh and cry at the same time, while Mrs. Webster stood there shouting, "Praise the Lord! Thank you, Jesus!"

When the excitement began to die down a little, Mrs. Webster took hold of my arm and said, "Come with me, Mr. Thom. There's someone you must meet."

I scrambled to my feet and went with her. She hooked her arm into mine and marched me down through the neighborhood and over to the Apostolic Faith Mission. The building was empty, except for two teenage girls who were playing the organ.

"Where's the pastor?" Mrs. Webster called out.

"He won't be in until later, Sister Webster," one of the girls replied.

"Good enough!" she said. "We'll wait."

It was about three in the afternoon. The girls resumed playing the organ, and the first thing I knew, they had me singing. I hadn't sung a hymn for a good many years, but once I got started, I couldn't stop. I "bellered out" all the songs I'd ever learned in Sunday school. After I'd sung every song I could think of, I started over. When the pastor finally came in at seven that evening, I was still going strong!

After Pastor Crompton heard my story, he knelt with me at the humble altar of that little mission and "prayed me through," as he said. He wanted to be sure I was "really saved," so I confessed my sins all over again and cried and laughed just like before, while Mrs. Webster shouted and praised the Lord.

When I finally stood to my feet, the pastor said, "Brother Thom, you'll never forget this day. You're a new person now, and I want you to be faithful to the Lord, and start coming to the Mission every service."

"I sure will, Pastor," I said gratefully, breaking into a broad smile. I knew something wonderful had happened to me.

After we had all shaken hands warmly, we parted and I began the walk home. . . .

Whatever made me stop off at the bar, I'll never know. Maybe it was just the natural thing to do. Maybe it hadn't yet dawned on me what had happened. Maybe I was wondering if you couldn't be a good Christian and still have an occasional drink. Maybe I was disgusted at myself for having promised that pastor I'd attend his sissified Mission. At any rate, by the time I got to the bar around eight-thirty, something made me go in.

I had two dollars and ten cents in my pocket, and beer was only nine cents a bottle in those days, so I ordered up a bottle. After finishing that off, I still felt sober, so I ordered something more expensive. A glass of wine. Then brandy. Then whiskey. First straight drinks, then mixed. By ten-thirty, I'd spent all the money I had.

I was getting ready to leave when an old friend of mine named Mostert came in and offered to buy me a drink. So I sat back down and he bought me drinks until eleven-thirty.

"Hey, Tommy," Mostert blurted out, "how come you aren't drunk? How come you're still sober?"

"Funny," I thought to myself. "I *am* sober!"

"What's the matter with you?" Mostert hollered. "Ain't my drinks good enough for you?"

"Oh, yeah," I replied. "They're good, all right!"

"Then why doncha get drunk with me? I oughta knock yer block off fer wastin' my money!"

He was a brute of a man, and I knew he could easily beat me up. So I quickly thanked him for the drinks and headed home. After three hours of drinking, I walked as straight as an arrow all the way home, and never felt a bit sick!

When I walked into my living room, there was

Mrs. Webster waiting for me! I felt so ashamed I wanted to run, but something held me.

"I've been waiting for you," she said. "I gave the children some supper, put them to bed and tidied up the house a bit." (The house was spotless.) "I thought I shouldn't leave the children until you came back," she explained. "Now, if you'll excuse me, I'll be on my way. Good night, Brother Thom."

As soon as the door closed, I breathed a sigh of relief. If she had guessed where I'd been, she never uttered a word about it.

"Dear God," I prayed in my bed that night, "I don't understand exactly what's happened to me today—and I don't understand how I drank all those drinks and didn't get drunk—but anyway, help me to start living right—and bless Joyce and the baby. Amen."

On Sunday morning, I got up knowing I had to find Joyce. I had a hunch that she'd gone to stay at her sister's place in another part of town, so I left Drummond with instructions to watch over the other kids while I went to get "Mommy."

On the way over to Joyce's sister's, I met a friend of mine who offered to buy me a drink. I can't say I really *wanted* it, but I was curious about the night before, and why I'd stayed sober. I wondered if it would work again. So I thanked my friend and he set me up to port wine and brandy, which is one of the most potent of all drinks.

I drank from nine o'clock that morning until two in the afternoon, and I stayed stone cold sober the whole time! I knew it had to be a miracle from God!

I thanked my friend for his hospitality, and

started off again to find Joyce. As I walked along steadily, I kept thinking, "*Something* really *went out* of me when that woman commanded those demons to leave me! I can't even get drunk! It's a miracle!" Then I began to think about the insatiable appetite for alcohol I'd had before she commanded that demon of alcohol to leave me. "Apparently," I thought, "that burning desire for alcohol wasn't merely a *human* desire. No. It was more than that. *What was I feeding* when I could drink sixteen quarts of beer in one night?" Whatever it was, it was gone.

By three o'clock Sunday afternoon, I arrived at Joyce's sister's place. Joyce and the baby were there. As I walked in the front door, my brother-in-law said, "Sorry, I haven't got a drink for you."

Squaring my shoulders and looking him straight in the eye, I said, "*I want to tell you, never again will I require yours or anybody else's drink. Thank you.*"

As I said those words, I felt a heavy burden slipping from my shoulders, like a wet Army overcoat falling to the ground. Jesus seemed to say to me, "*According to your faith be it unto you.*" I knew in that moment that I was free—that I was really saved.

Turning to Joyce, I said, "Woman, let's go home and start a new life." She gathered up the baby and said, "Well, all right—the kids probably need me."

On the way home, she asked, "What'd you mean back there about not drinking anymore?"

"Just what I said," I replied. "I've accepted Christ into my life and the old days are gone. No more liquor, no more cigarettes—nothing."

"Well, I've heard that story before," she said skeptically.

When we got home, she was surprised to find the house shining and the children dressed in their Sunday best. "Did you have your Sunday dinner yet?" she asked anxiously, hugging them all at once.

"Yes'm," they shouted. "We had a *special* dinner!"

"But who cooked it for you?"

"Mrs. Webster and the ladies from the church!"

"Mrs. Webster? The lady from the Apostolic Faith Mission?"

"Yes'm, and she got us all cleaned up, and the ladies cleaned up the house so you and Daddy wouldn't have nuthin' to do when you got home!"

"But why did Mrs. Webster come *here?*"

At that point, I broke in and explained the whole story to Joyce. "Oh, Bob!" she exclaimed, flinging her arms around my neck. "Then it's true! You're saved!" She laid her head on my shoulder and cried and cried. After a few minutes, she wiped the tears from her eyes. "I'm sorry I didn't have the courage to tell you, but I was saved last Sunday."

I drew back in astonishment. "*You're* saved?" I asked incredulously.

"Yes," she said shyly. "I was afraid to tell you, but I was hoping you'd notice the difference. . . ."

"I *did* notice," I replied, "but I had no idea what'd happened to you."

"Drummond accepted Jesus too."

"Drummond?"

"Yes."

"When?"

"On Easter Sunday."

"At the Mission?"

"No. At Mrs. Webster's children's meeting down at the beach."

"That crazy woman!" I said, chuckling. "She's out to get my whole family!"

"The sooner, the better!" Joyce replied, laughing.

"Let's all go to the Mission tonight," I suggested.

"I'd love that," Joyce said. "Just give me a few minutes to get ready."

While I was waiting, I picked up the Saturday paper which I hadn't read due to all the excitement of the day before. My eyes fell on an article about the black maid who'd been strangled to death down at the hotel bar the night I slept there. The article said the police had arrested her boy friend, and he had confessed to the murder. I dropped the paper on my lap, laid my head on the back of the chair and laughed and laughed. "Thank God!" I sighed. *"I didn't do it!"* I felt like I had been given a new lease on life.

A short time later, our whole family walked down to the Apostolic Faith Mission for the Sunday evening service. We filled up a whole pew. I enjoyed the singing and preaching, but the pastor's wife kept shouting "Hallelujah" and "Praise the Lord" all through the service, which bothered me a lot.

On the way home I said to Joyce, "I'll never go down there again. They're a bunch of fanatics!"

But on Wednesday evening we were back. And again on Friday. And again on Sunday. We began to enjoy the fellowship, and even the pastor's wife didn't seem so bad once we got to know her.

One of the big problems we faced after getting

started in the Christian life was our finances. I had spent so much money on booze that there had been little left to pay our bills. The indebtedness had piled up higher and higher, and as long as I was drinking, I didn't care. But now that I had come to Christ, I knew something had to be done. Joyce and I talked it over and we finally decided that we would begin by dedicating our whole family and its problems to the Lord. Hadn't Jesus said, "Seek ye first the kingdom of God, and his righteousness; and all these things shall be added unto you" (Matthew 6:33)? So we went down to the Mission the next Sunday and when the invitation was given, we all walked down the aisle and knelt at the altar. Joyce was holding the baby, and all our other blond-headed children were kneeling there reverently.

"Jesus," I said, "I've gotten my family into a terrible mess. I've wasted my money on drink, and the children haven't been properly fed or clothed, and the bills have gone unpaid." I wept like a child before going on. "Jesus, You've saved Joyce and me for the glory of Your name, and I believe You can straighten out all this mess if we'll just give it to You."

So I consecrated myself to the Lord, along with my wife and children. I told God He could have all my children to be missionaries, if that's what He wanted. I told Him about my asthmatic condition which had been getting steadily worse ever since the orphanage days. I told Him about my failures and frustrations. I told Him about my debts—the thousands of dollars which I knew I couldn't pay. I had two very large loans from the Navy and the Military War Fund, in addition to my rent, food, clothing and other expenses. "God," I prayed, "I give you these debts in the name of Jesus."

I didn't know it then, but when you give a debt to God, it becomes *His* debt—and God always pays His debts! Three weeks later, I received two identical letters from both funds saying that, after meetings with the committees, my loans had been converted to grants, and there would be no need to repay them!

CHAPTER SIX

"J-JESUS THE HEALER AND B-BAPTIZER"

Nineteen forty-eight was a big year. I was still in the Navy, but since my conversion a year and a half before, I had been devoting most of my free time to Bible study and helping out down at the Mission. I was growing spiritually, but a big test was just around the corner that I knew nothing about.

I had discovered that one of the doctrines which was continually emphasized at the Mission was that of divine healing. The pastor stoutly proclaimed that Jesus was able to heal all our sicknesses, and I believed him. Our choir director also frequently spoke of God's healing power. Time and again, I saw sick people being anointed with oil, according to the instructions in James 5:14. Each time, the pastor would quote Mark 16:18: ". . . they shall lay hands on the sick, and they shall recover."

But no one ever recovered. No one was ever healed. This was very disheartening to me. My asthmatic condition was getting worse. Over and over again, I would wake during the night with a start, gasping for my breath. I had been anointed and anointed, but nothing ever happened.

So one evening I went to the choir director and said, "Isn't there *anybody* around this town who can pray for my healing? I'm *sick!*"

"Well," she said, "I'll pray for you, if you want me to."

"But you *have* prayed for me," I countered, "and I'm sicker than ever."

"I know," she said with a far-away look in her eyes. "You should have been around when John G. Lake was here."

"Why? Who's John G. Lake?"

"Oh, he's the American preacher who did all the miracles when he was here—but he's gone back to the United States now. . . ."

"And took the miracles with him," I added sarcastically.

"Well, Brother Thom," she replied, "there's nobody else around here who can pray the prayer of faith like *he* did."

"I've noticed that," I replied sadly.

I went home that night disgusted and discouraged. I'm sure Joyce must have noticed. Before going to bed, I took two ephedrine tablets, which was the only thing that gave me relief from my labored breathing. I sat down on the edge of the bed, picked up my Bible from the nightstand, and opened it at random to the Gospel of Mark. There I read these words:

> *For verily I say unto you, That whosoever shall say unto this mountain, Be thou removed, and be thou cast into the sea; and shall not doubt in his heart, but shall believe that those things which he saith shall come to pass; he shall have whatsoever he saith* (Mark 11:23).

"Lord," I said, "is that promise for me? Or was that only for the twelve disciples?"

"*Read it again*," the Holy Spirit seemed to say.

So I began again, this time uttering the words under my breath. "*For verily I say unto you, That whosoever. . . .*" I stopped dead. *Whosoever!* "Lord," I exclaimed, "that means this promise is for *anybody* who chooses to believe it!"

Then the thought crossed my mind that perhaps this promise applied only to certain situations. Maybe it had nothing to do with my sickness—or anybody else's sickness. So I read the remainder of the verse, and the Holy Spirit let me "see" the last few words of the verse: "*. . . he shall have whatsoever he saith.*" *Whatsoever. Whatsoever!* Anything—*anything* in the whole wide world—is possible where there is faith.

Whosoever and whatsoever! Anybody can have anything, if he'll just believe! The promise was so big it almost made my head swim. "Lord," I prayed, "if nobody else in this town has made this Bible come alive since John G. Lake was here, then let me be the first!"

A few days later, I was back down at the Mission, and for some strange reason, I felt urged to begin praying for the sick. It was strange. I was still suffering with my asthma, and it didn't make any sense that I, a sick man, should be ministering to the sick—but this seemed to be what God was telling me to do; so at the close of the service, I prayed for a few sick people. Within several days, much to my surprise, I heard that they were well.

Encouraged, I began to pray for the sick more regularly. Often I would visit sick friends in their homes and offer prayer for them. God began to work miracles. A few outstanding healings were written up in the local newspaper. But still I wheezed on. I just couldn't understand why God wouldn't heal me.

I experienced a temporary lull in my discouragement the day the pastor asked me if I'd preach the sermon on the following Sunday evening.

"Do you think I can do it, Pastor?" I asked anxiously.

"Aren't you a sailor in the South African Navy?" he retorted.

"Yessir."

"And aren't you in partnership with God Almighty?"

"Yessir."

"Then you'll *do* it, my man—you'll do it!"

I grinned and thanked him for the honor.

On the way home, I decided to stop off and see Brother Busche, who was one of the elders of our Mission. "Guess what?" I blurted out, as I walked into the living room where he was sitting. "I'm preaching on Sunday night!"

"Oh, is that so?" he replied in surprise. "And how come *you're* preaching?"

"The pastor invited me," I replied with a wide smile.

"Well, isn't that nice?" he said coldly, with a trace of jealousy. "I suppose you're expecting to have a great service?"

"Well," I said, "there'll be some souls saved, I'm sure of that."

"But what makes you so sure?" he asked. "Don't you know that outside of your being won to the Lord by Mrs. Webster, we haven't seen a soul saved in four years?"

"That might be so," I replied, "but you come on Sunday night, and you'll see."

"Brother Thom," he said, standing to his feet indignantly, "do you think God would bypass us elders and deacons and work through a novice?"

"I didn't mean any disrespect. . . ." I stammered.

"Get out of my house!" he shouted. "Your pride is an abomination to God!"

"Okay, I'm sorry," I said, turning to leave. "But you come on Sunday night; you'll see."

On Sunday night he was there, acting very cool. But God helped me preach my message and sure enough, four people came forward to be saved. Realizing how wrong he had been, Brother Busche came to me after the service and asked to be forgiven. However, due to criticism from some of the other elders and deacons, the pastor was much more careful about asking me to preach after that.

But regardless, I felt my responsibility to be a witness for Christ whenever possible, so I began going down to the beach on Sunday afternoons and witnessing to the people there. It never occurred to me that that's where all the Jewish people went on Sunday! Needless to say, my testimony was scorned and ridiculed.

There was little encouragement from anyone except Joyce. Most of the people at the Mission kept telling me, "Be careful, you're going too fast." But it didn't seem sensible to slow down in my zeal for the Lord. I'd lost too much time already in the years I'd lived in sin.

Walking down the street some time later, I met Danny Maxwell, the Sunday school superintendent in the Methodist church where I had previously been a member. This man had helped bring me home one night when I was dead drunk, just two months before my conversion, so I was sure he'd be overjoyed to hear my testimony.

After I told him about the wonderful change in my life, he said, "Well, I'm glad to hear about the change in you, but I don't think I've seen you in church. Where've you been?"

"Oh," I said, "you see, this Mrs. Webster who led me to Christ took me down to the Apostolic Faith Mission and introduced me to the pastor, and I've been going there ever since."

"*You're* attending the *Apostolic Faith Mission?*" he asked in disdain.

"Yes. Been attending there for a year and a half now."

"You're a member?"

"Sure."

He shook his head in disbelief. "Tommy, I never thought I'd see the day when you'd leave the Methodist Church and get mixed up in a false sect. If you want to know the truth, you were better off when you were drinking."

I left him, stunned. As I walked home, I kept repeating to myself, "Imagine! He'd rather have me be a drunken Methodist than a saved Christian attending that Mission!" I just couldn't understand it.

But even more discouraging was what happened on the following Saturday. Pastor Crompton and his wife knew how I was suffering with my asthma, and when they heard about a certain Brother McQuade who was to speak and minister to the sick at the Apostolic Faith Church in Plumstead, they decided to take Joyce and me to the meeting.

"Who knows?" Pastor Crompton said optimistically. "You might come back a well man!"

"I sure hope so," I replied. "I can't go on like this much longer."

But what a disappointment it was when Brother McQuade stood up to speak! He was a humpbacked man, badly deformed, with bony hands and hawk-like features. "How can *that* man minister to the sick?" I asked myself. "He's half dead himself!"

To make matters worse, when he opened his mouth to speak, he stuttered terribly. He said he was going to talk about "J-Jesus the Healer and B-Baptizer in the S-S-Spirit."

I sat there and listened to him stuttering and thought to myself, "That man is a liar; if he's got any healing power, why doesn't he use some of it on himself?"

I left that meeting more discouraged than ever.

By the following Wednesday, I was just about licked. The asthma was acting up more than usual that day, so I reported off work. I wheezed and gasped for breath until I was completely exhausted.

"Why don't you go over to the pastor's house?" Joyce suggested. "They're having a prayer meeting this morning."

"That's a good idea," I agreed. "Maybe I can get healed today."

"Well, I sure hope so," she said. "If God doesn't do something about that asthma, you'll soon be off work *every* day."

So I walked over to Pastor Crompton's home and joined the group that was already assembled in his living room. I soon found that it was just a regular prayer meeting where the people were praying for revival and for the needs of the Mission.

After the close of the meeting, I continued kneeling at my chair, praying aloud for God's healing touch for my asthma. Most of the people went home, but when Sister Crompton heard me praying, she laid her hand on my shoulder and prayed, "Lord, help this brother in his self-pity."

"Self-pity!" I snorted to myself. "She doesn't understand what I've been through lately!" Just then, there was a knock at the door, and she went to answer.

A few minutes later, the pastor came from upstairs where he'd gone after the meeting, laid his hand on my head and prayed, "Please, Father, help this brother in his self-pity!"

"What's going on here?" I asked myself. "They've rehearsed *that* prayer!"

Then another person asked to speak to the pastor, so he left me. A thought popped into my mind from somewhere: "They don't love you."

"That's right," I agreed, "they never *did*."

I quit praying, and began rehearsing all my doubts and troubles to myself.

"Might as well face up to the facts," I thought. "They *talk* about healing, but they don't have any more healing power than this chair I'm leaning on. They talk about love, but I can't do *anything* down at that Mission anymore because of their carnal jealousy!"

I knelt there in silence for a long time, as though trying to summon courage to think my *real* thoughts. Finally, I could hold them back no longer: "God doesn't care anything about me. If He did, He'd heal me. He'd lift me up. He'd help me understand the Bible better than I do. He'd give me more power to witness. But He doesn't care. I was crazy to ever believe in this stuff. I'm nothing but a dumb hypocrite. Just like the rest of them. . . ."

I got up from the chair where I was kneeling, tiptoed out the front door without saying goodbye to anyone, and caught a bus. I was so disgusted that I could have ended it all right there. A thought came to me from somewhere: "Why don't you go back to the Grand Hotel where you used to drink?"

"Might as well," I muttered in the depths of despair. "Nobody cares anyhow."

About a block from the Hotel, I pulled the buzzer, signaling the driver that I wanted to get off. As I stood to leave the bus, I heard a voice, not quite audible, but nevertheless very distinct. The voice said, "*I will never leave thee nor forsake thee.*" I stepped off the bus, crossed the street, and again heard the voice, "*I will never leave thee nor forsake thee.*"

By the time I got to the Grand Hotel, there was Jock the bartender out on the sidewalk, right where the devil had planted him! As I passed, Jock recognized me.

"Tommy! Old buddy!" he cried, breaking into a broad smile. "What a long time it's been since I've seen *you!* Come on in and have a drink on the house!" It was like Satan's hot breath right in my face.

"Can't come in today, Jock," I replied with a burst of determination, and kept on walking. As I walked faster and faster, I received the strangest impression to go to the home of Brother McQuade, and he would tell me about the baptism of the Holy Ghost. I knew I needed a baptism of something or other, so I went.

I was pretty sure McQuade lived somewhere up the hill beyond the big Groot Schuur Hospital, so I caught a bus—but it turned out to be the wrong one. Not wanting to spend any more money on buses, I walked all the way up the hill, inquiring for McQuade's house as I went.

By one o'clock, I still hadn't found it, and I was hungry, so I spent my last bit of change on a chocolate candy bar, full of nuts and raisins. I unwrapped it and was about to bite into it when I noticed that it was wormy. Disgusted, I dropped it into the gutter. A voice seemed to say, "God's not even interested in you when you're hungry." For a moment I thought about turning around and going back home. But then I remembered that other voice, "*I will never leave you. . . .*"

Finally, I found McQuade's house. I knocked and a maid came to the door.

"My name is Thom—Robert Thom," I said.

"Yes, Mr. Thom. Who do you want to see?"

"Brother McQuade. Is he here?"

"Yes. Come in. He'll see you right after lunch." She took my jacket and disappeared into the next room.

I sat down to wait. But when I began to think about talking to McQuade about the Holy Ghost, I wasn't sure I wanted to go through with it. I felt like getting up and sneaking out the door. But just then, old stoop-shouldered McQuade came into the room where I was sitting.

"Oh, B-Brother Tommy!" he said with a shriveled-up smile. "What can I d-do for you?"

Looking for a way out, I said, "Well, er, I've got sinus trouble," which I did. With no hesitation, he came over to me, clamped that bony hand over

82

my nose and said, "In the name of Jesus Christ, thou spirit of sinus, *leave him!*" In that moment, some strange power came over me and my nostrils opened up completely. I took a big gulp of fresh air and said, "Praise the Lord!"

"Brother," he said, "kneel d-down, you need the Holy G-Ghost."

"Actually," I stammered, "that's what I came for."

"I knew it," he replied with a twinkle in his eye. "Kneel down here and begin to p-praise God. G-God's going to b-baptize you in the Holy Ghost."

Obediently, I knelt down and tried to praise God for all He had done for me. But my mouth was dry, and my heart wasn't in it.

While I was kneeling there, I "heard" a voice say to me, "Your house is on fire! Your wife is calling!"

Jumping to my feet, I said to McQuade, "Where's my jacket?"

"Why, wh-what's wrong?"

"My house is on fire and my wife is calling me!"

He looked at me strangely for a moment, then turned on his heel and opened a window. "You d-devil," he shouted, pointing to the open window, "in the name of Jesus Christ, g-*get out of here!*"

Then, turning to me, he said, "Brother, your wife n-n-never called you, and your house isn't on f-fire." Then, as he closed the window and locked it, he explained, "That was a d-demon opposing you. But I have c-commanded him to leave in the name of J-Jesus, and he has obeyed. Now let's get b-back to the b-business at hand."

I knew very little about this "demon" business, and wasn't sure that I *wanted* to either! Issuing commands to invisible devils and spirits was a little far out for me. Yet I remembered how Mrs. Webster had cast the "drinking demon" out of me, whatever that was, so perhaps there was something to it.

"Now, Brother Tommy," McQuade went on, "God d-doesn't want lip service, He wants p-praise from the heart. If you really want to be b-baptized in the Holy Ghost, then start p-praising God with all your heart. F-Faith thrives in praise, and God lives in the praises of His p-people."

So I raised my hands and began to praise God with all my heart. The dryness left my mouth. My tongue felt like it was on fire, as praise began to pour out of me. Suddenly, I was caught up in the Spirit. It was strange—a sort of "out-of-the-body" experience, when my spirit seemed to be seeing into another realm.

I saw a white marble staircase coming down out of heaven. It folded down like an accordion, and rested on the ground before me. Then I saw a miniature man on his knees at the bottom of that great staircase, looking up and clapping his hands in adoration and praise. I was amazed when I saw the little man looked exactly like *me!*

Fascinated by this little man so caught up in worship, my eyes traveled up the staircase to see the object of his gaze. The first thing I observed was a pair of nail-pierced feet, wearing sandals, and stepping down through the clouds which obscured the top of the staircase. Knowing it was the Lord, I bowed my head in awe, as His footsteps came ever closer.

When I lifted my eyes again, I gasped in wonder. He appeared as a great, strong Man clothed in a silverish-white robe, tied with a broad golden sash. His ruddy face radiated light like the sun. In His right hand, He carried a large, narrow-necked pitcher full of new wine.

I instantly remembered how Jesus had said, "If any man thirst, let him come unto me, and drink" (John 7:37). I also recalled John's explanation of that statement in verse 39: "But this spake he of the Spirit which they that believe on him should receive. . . ."

As soon as the Lord reached the bottom of the staircase, He spoke to that little man who, I now knew, was me. *"My son,"* He said, *"I now give you the gift of faith."* And I saw that little man cup his tiny hands, and the Lord poured sparkling wine into them, and the man drank.

Then the Lord said, *"My son, I also give you the gift of healing."* And again He tipped the pitcher and poured more wine into those little hands. And again the man drank.

A third time the Lord spoke. He said, *"I give you the gift of prophecy."* More wine was poured. And the man drank.

A fourth time, the Lord said, *"I give you the word of knowledge."* The wine gurgled from the pitcher, and the man drank.

A fifth time, the Lord said, *"I give you the gift of tongues."* I saw the little man drink as before, and suddenly he looked up at the Lord, as though he would burst for joy. (I remember thinking at the same time, "If I don't open my mouth now, and let this that's *in* me *out*, I'm going to blow up!" I felt like the "Dunlap tire man"—the little cartoon character the Dunlap Company employed in those days to advertise their tires—a little fat man made of tires and tubes. I was so full of joy and worship, I couldn't contain it!) Suddenly the little man began to worship the Lord in a language I had never heard before. At first it was hesitating and stumbling, but then it became a clear dialect, sweet and full of worship. As I watched this little man praising the Lord, suddenly the marble staircase swung away to the left and disappeared. Then I saw the Lord vanish into thin air, and the little figure vanished too. For a few moments I seemed to "come back down to earth" and found myself on my knees in Brother McQuade's front room, praying in tongues! What *rivers* of living water were flowing out of me! I knew the Lord had baptized me in the Holy Spirit.

But quickly, I was caught up in the Spirit again. This time, I looked up and saw a four-square city gracefully lowering itself to the earth, like a majestic spaceship.

As the city came down slowly, I was caught up high into the heavens, where I was able to see the breath-taking beauty of this Heavenly Metropolis. For size, it was like seeing a hundred New York Cities combined into one great city. I could see the beautiful roofs of gold, and the park-like areas where trees arched over the streets.

Again I was swished out far to the east of the city. Looking back, I was surprised to see a Man on a white horse, between me and the city. He must have been almost sixteen feet tall, and was strong and muscular, with golden bands around His arms.

"Lord," I cried out, "why is the Christ so big?"

And I heard a voice boom out of the city which said, "*He is no longer the babe of Bethlehem, no longer the crucified Christ—but now the King of*

Kings and Lord of Lords, coming back to receive the redeemed of all ages."

Instantly the vision vanished. When I came to myself, I was still worshipping in tongues. McQuade was laughing and praising the Lord at the same time. I stood to my feet, staggered out of that house drunk on the "wine" of the Spirit, and didn't even tell McQuade goodbye. All I can remember is his hilarious laughter as I walked out his front door.

When I got home that afternoon, Joyce said, "Well, how was the prayer meeting?"

"Oh, great!" I replied. "I'm not healed yet, but I think I can go on now."

"Good!" she said happily, as she set the table for supper. "I was praying something extra good would happen to you today."

"It did!" I said, smiling.

CHAPTER SEVEN

THE HOUSE WITH MANY FRUIT TREES

It was in that same year that the Navy transferred me up to the Transvaal (the northeast province of South Africa), almost a thousand miles away. It wasn't easy to leave Joyce and the children, but we had committed our lives to Christ, and we knew He was in control of every situation we faced.

I was stationed in Pretoria, which is the capital city of the Transvaal. While there I tried to take advantage of every opportunity to witness for Christ. The weekends were free, so I had plenty of time to share Christ with anybody who would listen.

One weekend, God brought to my mind the Full Gospel Church in Benoni and told me I was to preach there on Sunday morning. "Lord," I protested, "it's not good etiquette to walk into a church and tell them you're there to preach!"

"*Trust Me,*" the Lord seemed to say. "*There is one there who needs your help.*"

So early Sunday morning I donned my sailor's dress uniform, and with a dime in my pocket, I hitchhiked down to that church, which was many miles away. When I arrived, the people treated me very nicely, and asked all about me. When they found out that I'd come all the way from Pretoria just to be in their service, they were puzzled. "Why would you hitchhike all the way down here to be in our church?" they asked.

"Well, er—ah—you probably won't believe this, but God sent me down here to preach this morning."

Quickly, two of them went to the pastor and told him about me and what I'd said. When the time came for the church service, I found myself behind the pulpit, preaching! And, oh, how they enjoyed the simple Gospel message I preached!

Remembering what the Lord had said about someone I was to help, I kept watching for my target—but by the end of the service I still hadn't spotted my prospect. I was a little disappointed.

However, after the service a Brother and Sister Anderson asked me if I'd go home with them and pray for their daughter, Hope, who had muscular dystrophy. I agreed to go, and they took me out to their corn farm. Oscar Changuoin, who was secretary to the General Manager of the South African Railways in Johannesburg and a great soul winner, went along.

As soon as I saw young Hope, I knew she was the person I'd been sent to help. She was horribly crippled, and one of her legs was drawn and paralysed.

"Hope," I said, taking her by the hand, "Jesus is going to heal you today." Then I knelt down with Oscar and Brother and Sister Anderson, and we prayed a simple prayer of faith, and proceeded to praise the Lord for the answer even before we saw any visible evidence of a healing.

Later that day, I hitchhiked back to Pretoria. Oscar assured me that he would call as soon as there was any visible change in Hope's condition. Actually, I expected to get his call that night. But no call came.

So I waited all day Monday, but still I heard nothing. By Monday evening, my mind was flooded with questions about the reality of my faith, and why I wasn't seeing more immediate results.

On Tuesday morning, the phone rang. It was Oscar. "Brother Thom!" he shouted into the receiver. "Did you hear what happened to Hope Anderson?"

"No," I replied, smiling and holding the phone away from my ear, "what happened?"

"She woke up Monday morning and she was *perfectly healed!*"

"You mean all the paralysis is gone?"

"Every bit of it!"

"And has her leg straightened out? And has it been lengthened?"

"Yes, it's straightened out and it's been lengthened by two and a half inches!"

"She's walking then?"

"Walking! They can't get her to sit down!"

"Praise the Lord!" I shouted.

"Amen!" Oscar replied, sobbing.

I hung up the receiver, overwhelmed at the reality of God's healing power. A few weeks later I hitchhiked out to Benoni especially to see Hope for myself. I could hardly believe it was the same girl.*

* The reader will be interested to know that four or five years after this healing, Hope Anderson applied for a Civil Service job. In order to complete her physical examination, the attending physician asked for her medical history. The doctor who had attended her during her illness had passed on, but they were able to obtain the records from the local hospital. When the doctor had laid out her medical history

It was then that I realized the importance of *acting* in faith. There was no visible reason why we should have praised the Lord for healing Hope when we first prayed for her. The visible evidence said, "No, she's not healed." But I also knew the Bible said that "faith without works is dead" (James 2:20). That's why we decided to put our faith into action and praise God in advance. We chose to believe God's promises even more than we believed the circumstances we saw with our eyes. Didn't the Bible say that "faith is . . . the evidence of *things not seen*" (Hebrews 11:1)? This was the principle which was to become the key to the exciting life of faith God had mapped out for me. In fact, it was only a few days later that I was to use this key again.

When it began to appear that I would be stationed in Pretoria for some time, I began to pray that God would make it possible for me to move my family up from Cape Town. I missed Joyce a great deal, and the kids needed their father. But there was an acute housing shortage. I knew it would be next to impossible to find a place to live—unless God worked a miracle.

One Sunday night when I was praying very ear-

---

sheets, and re-examined her, he said, "Was your doctor in his right mind? He must have been mental."

"Why do you say that?" Hope asked.

"These records show that you had muscular dystrophy—but you're in perfect health."

"True," she said, "I'm in perfect health *now*, but I *did* have dystrophy."

"Then what happened?" the doctor asked.

"Well," she said, "a man prayed for me. . . ."

She got the job, and is now married to the pastor of a Full Gospel Church of God in South Africa. She continues to enjoy good health.

nestly about this, an overpowering impression came to me that God was going to give me a home with many fruit trees. I was so sure it was God speaking to me that I went down to the Government Housing Control Office on Monday and applied for a house. After filling out the form, I returned it to the lady at the desk.

"Madam," I said, "I am going down to Cape Town to get my family. We'll be back Friday night. As soon as you get the key for my house, will you kindly leave it at this address?" And I handed her a slip of paper bearing the name and address of the pastor whose church I had been attending since being in Pretoria.

She looked at me like I was stark raving mad. "Sir," she said, "it may interest you to know that you are number 11,001 on the housing list. I'm afraid it's impossible."

"No," I said insistently, "*God told me* He was going to give me a house with many fruit trees."

"Sir," she replied, "you can't bribe me."

"Madam, I'm not bribing you," I replied, smiling. "I'm just telling you that you will leave the key with this man, and I'm moving in. We'll be arriving Friday night."

As she stared at me speechlessly, I turned and left her standing there with my form in her hand. But she was no more amazed than I was! As I walked away from that desk, I marveled at my own audacity in declaring my faith with such certainty. "Where did I ever get faith like *that?*" I asked myself in bafflement.

When I got back to Cape Town, Joyce and the kids were surprised to see me—and doubly surprised to learn that we were moving!

"But I don't have anything packed!" Joyce said.

"It won't take long," I said. "If we all pitch in, we can have everything ready in a day."

She looked at me half angry and half amused. Suddenly she burst out in rollicking laughter. "Bob," she said, "you're the craziest man I ever met!"

By the end of the day, we had everything packed, and I made arrangements to have it all trucked over to the rail freight office the first thing next morning. By mid-morning on Thursday, we were on board the train, clickety-clacking on our way up to Pretoria. The kids were tired from the day before and soon fell asleep.

"Well, it surely feels good to relax a little," Joyce said, leaning her blond head against the pullman seat.

"Yes, that was *some* day yesterday, wasn't it?" I replied, yawning.

Suddenly, she sat straight up and said, "Bob, you never *did* tell me about our new home."

"Oh, yes," I replied. "In all the hurry, I forgot to tell you. You'll love it. It's got lots of fruit trees."

"How many bedrooms?"

"Enough."

"Does it have a nice sized kitchen?"

"You'll like it, I'm sure."

"Is that all you can say?"

"I wanted it to be a surprise."

"Oh." She smiled, and again laid her head back against the seat. It wasn't long until she was sleeping peacefully.

"Lord," I prayed under my breath, "if You fail me now, I'll never speak to You again."

Friday evening around six o'clock, we arrived in

Pretoria. As soon as we got off the train, I went to a phone and called the pastor.

"This is Robert Thom," I said. "Do you have any word for me?"

"Oh, yes, Robert," he said. "A woman stopped by today and left a key for you—and a slip of paper with an address on it."

"What's the address?" I asked, pulling out my pen.

"Forty Van Heerden Street, Capital Park, Pretoria."

"Thank you," I said. "I'll be right over to get the key."

Before leaving the telephone, I quickly made another call, arranging to have our belongings taken to our new address.

When we arrived at the new house, the first thing I noticed was that it was surrounded with fruit trees! Tears filled my eyes. I unlocked the front door of the house, and Joyce and the kids squealed in delight. While they were investigating, I went out in the yard and counted fourteen varieties of fruit trees—apricots, peaches, apples, pears, oranges, lemons, pomegranates, figs, prickly pears and others. This had to be a miracle.

"Jesus," I said with a lump in my throat, "why are You so good to us?"

CHAPTER EIGHT

HITCHHIKING A THOUSAND MILES

About six months later, another one of those strange impressions came to me: I would be going back to Cape Town soon. But since we were just getting nicely settled in Pretoria, I couldn't understand why it should be so soon. Knowing the danger of blindly following every notion that comes along, I began to pray for special guidance.

Soon the impression became even more clear. God seemed to be saying to me, *"You must fast and pray for fourteen days. You will soon be leaving your family for a brief time, and going back to Cape Town. There I will show you another part of My plan for you."*

Going to Capetown was very appealing to me. One of my dearest Christian friends, Ken Sawyer, lived there. If I could just spend a few days of fasting and prayer in the quietness of Ken's home, I was sure God would make His will known to me.

I was due for a thirty-day leave starting the following week, and it seemed this would be my only opportunity to make the trip for some time. So I told Joyce about God's dealing with me, and she agreed that I should go.

The next day I began fasting. I had decided it should be a total fast, except for water. So, at each mealtime, I prayed instead of eating, usually in some private place where I could concentrate on Jesus.

By the fifth day, I knew the time had come for me to start my journey. I had only a little change in my pocket, but I felt confident that the Lord would make a way. So I bade my family goodbye and started off on the thousand-mile trip.

I got a ride over to the Zwartskop Airport, on a hunch that perhaps I could hitchhike a ride on a plane. It was easy for servicemen to hitchhike on almost anything in those days. When I told the officer in charge what I wanted, he glanced at my Navy uniform and said, "Where are you going?"

"Cape Town, sir."

"Hitchhiking all the way?"

"Yes, sir."

"We've got a plane leaving in an hour. Just sign these forms and you've got a ride."

"What do I have to pay?"

"How much do you have on you?"

"Eighty cents."

He grinned. "You planning on coming back?"

"Yes, sir."

"Okay, if the round trip costs eighty cents, then half fare will be forty cents." He stamped my papers, tore off my copy and handed it to me.

I thanked him, saluted, and walked over to the hangar where the plane was being serviced. In a short time, the old military plane roared down the airstrip, and I was on my way.

Instead of going directly to Cape Town, which was due south, the pilot turned the plane eastward. "We've got to make a stop out on the coast," he explained. "We'll have a layover tonight, and tomorrow we'll head south to East London. We're due in Cape Town the day after that."

So that evening, we landed at an airport out on the coast. Having a little free time on my hands, I decided to see if I couldn't find a good Gospel meeting to attend somewhere. I finally did locate a little hall where a missionary was trying to preach to some Hindus. It was sad to see what spiritual darkness they were in. As I sat there watching that missionary working with those people, God seemed to say to me, "*There are many such as these who do not know Me, nor My power. Obey Me, and I will show you an open door of ministry.*"

Later on, I had a pleasant conversation with the missionary; when he learned that I was on my way to Cape Town, he offered me a room for the night, which I accepted with gratitude.

The next morning, I was on the plane again, flying down the coast to East London. "We'll have a little rough weather," the pilot remarked. "East London radio says it's been pouring rain down there for almost twenty-four hours now with no sign of a letup." But the twin engines droned on for most of the day, and the flying was perfect.

Late that afternoon, however, about a half hour before we were due to land, we ran into bad weather. The plane bumped along through the clouds like an old bus traveling a country road. Within minutes, we found ourselves in a slashing rain storm.

Fifteen or twenty minutes later, the pilot tried to radio the airport for landing instructions, but couldn't get through.

"What's the trouble?" I asked.

"The blamed radio must be burned out," he replied in disgust. "We'll have to go in blind."

I looked out the window and couldn't see a thing. There was nothing out there but a world of rain and clouds. It was the sixth day of my fast. "Lord," I prayed under my breath, "I refuse to worry; my life is in Your hands."

In a few minutes, we broke through a very low ceiling, and through the relentless rain we could make out the obscure layout of a city below. The pilot circled carefully two or three times, trying to spot the airstrip.

"I've got it!" he said in a moment. "Hold on to your hat; here we go!"

I praised the Lord all the way down. Within minutes, we were taxiing down the wet runway, safe and sound.

"Why don't you try to get a lift down to Cape Town some other way?" the pilot suggested. "I have a hunch we're going to have a long layover here. The weather report says nothing but rain, rain, rain for the next few days. We'll never be able to take off in weather like this."

"Okay, thanks," I replied. "I'll see what I can do."

The airport was on the outskirts of East London. It was getting late in the day, and I needed to find a place to sleep, so I hitchhiked a ride into a residential section of town. When I got out of the car it was still pouring, so I dashed into the doorway of a little store to keep dry, and prayed for guidance. As I prayed, my attention was drawn to a little house up the street. Bolting up the street through the blinding rain, I went straight for that house and banged on the door. A kind-faced woman answered.

"Goodness, come in!" she said. "You'll be soaked!"

"Thank you, ma'am," I replied, stepping inside. "You're very kind."

"And who might *you* be?" she asked curiously.

"Robert Thom, ma'am. I'm traveling from Pretoria to Cape Town."

"And you're in the Navy?"

"Yes, but I'm on leave."

"But, whatever made you come to *my* house?"

"Well, I guess I was *led* here. You see, I'm a child of God."

"You are? You're a born-again Christian?"

"Yes, ma'am."

"Well, then, let me feed you. What would you like to eat?"

"Will you be offended if I decline, ma'am? You see, I'm not eating today."

"You're not? Then what would you like to drink?"

"Just a glass of cold water."

"Cold water? Are you fasting?"

"Yes."

"How amazing that you should come to my door," she replied. "I have fasted many, many times. One time I fasted for forty-five days. I've seen great answers to prayer through fasting. In fact, when my husband got disgusted and left the ministry, I prayed him back into the ministry through fasting."

"Your husband's a minister?" I asked in surprise.

"Oh, yes!" she said. "He's the pastor of the Full Gospel Church here in East London. In fact, we'll be having a service there tonight. Would you like to come along?"

"I'd like that, Mrs.—"

"Stevens—I'm sorry, I got carried away. Did you say you wanted *cold* water?"

"Yes, ma'am."

"No," she said kindly, "when you fast, you should drink *warm* water."

"Really?"

"Yes, it will help keep you warmer, and will eliminate the poisons from your body more quickly. You won't have half the headaches that people sometimes get from fasting, either."

"I never knew that."

"It's true. I'll heat a cup for you. By the way, you can stay with us tonight." She filled the kettle and set it on the stove. "Now, tell me," she continued, "whatever made you decide to follow the Lord?"

So I shared my testimony with her. I told her all about the orphanage days and my drinking problem and how the Lord had delivered me and baptized me in the Spirit. She listened with great interest.

"What a wonderful testimony!" she exclaimed. "You should tell this story in our church!" Sure enough, when her husband came home an hour later, she told him all about my testimony and he agreed to let me speak.

The next morning, I awoke early. It was still raining. I dreaded getting out in that foul weather again, but I had to get to Cape Town. There was an old Bible on a little table next to my bed. I swung my feet out of the bed and picked it up. Apparently it had been a child's Bible many years before. Inside the front cover, I found these words scrawled in childish handwriting:

God is love.
God sends the rain.

When I read that, I felt ashamed of myself. "For-give me, Lord," I prayed. "How could I be so un-grateful? You've led me on this journey, You've brought me to friends, You've given me shelter and You've protected me. And even the rain is a gift of Your love."

"*Continue on your way today,*" the Lord seemed to say. "*As you go, you will hear a voice behind you saying, This is the way; walk ye in it.*"

So I got dressed, went downstairs to thank the Stevens for their kindness, and stepped out into the pelting rain.

Down the street a short distance, I found a shelter where I could stand until I was able to get a ride. Finally, a car stopped.

"Where to?" the driver shouted, winding the window down a little.

"Cape Town."

"Not going that far," he replied. "Will Port Eliz-abeth help?" That was several hundred miles down the coast.

"It sure will!" I exclaimed.

"Then come on and get in."

I hopped in and after about 100 miles, we finally drove out of the rain.

That evening, I found myself in another minis-ter's home. This minister had formerly been a Navy commander, and he was greatly interested in my story. As I shared with him how God had worked in my life, he said, "Why don't you tell that story in my church tonight?" So for the second night in a row, God gave me an opportunity to preach the Gospel. That night, the pastor gave me a bed and the dollar and forty cent offering.

The next morning I was out on the road again. The weather was good, so I walked a short distance until I came to a place called Green Acres Hotel. They had a bar there so I took a notion to go in and see if I could testify to anybody.

When I walked in, I discovered they were just opening up. In fact, the counter was still lined with beer glasses from the night before, some empty, some half full.

"Can I help you, buddy?" the bartender spoke up.

"How far to Cape Town?" I asked.

"About 500 miles. You hitchhiking?"

"Yes. I guess I've got a long trip ahead of me yet."

"Yeah, how about a drink for the road?"

"No, thanks," I said. "I don't drink anymore. Had my fill of it."

"Nobody ever gets their fill of booze, buddy."

"*I* did. You know, just a few years back, I'd have drained every glass in this place."

"You *would* have? What happened to you?"

"I got saved."

"Saved?" he spat out. "What do you mean?"

So I told him. The whole story. I talked and talked. After I'd sowed all the Gospel seed in that man's mind that I could think of, something unusual happened.

A vision appeared in front of me. It was so real, it was uncanny. It was like a dream, excepting the fact that my eyes were wide open. I saw a green Pontiac driving toward the Green Acres Hotel. I saw myself standing beside the road hitchhiking.

102

Soon the green Pontiac came along, stopped, and took me all the way to Cape Town. Then as suddenly as it appeared, the vision vanished.

It scared me. I decided that God was trying to tell me to get on my way, so I said to the bartender, "Well, I'd better go now; a green Pontiac is going to pick me up and take me to Cape Town."

"Oh, you've arranged for somebody to pick you up?"

"No—God just told me a green Pontiac is coming."

"You must be joking."

"No, I'm not joking."

"You're crazy then."

"No, I'd better go. That Pontiac is coming now."

"Is it?" he said, looking at me doubtfully.

"Yes!" I shouted, dashing down the walk toward the gate. It was about a hundred yards to the road. Just as I stepped through that gate, a green Pontiac stopped!

"Where are you going?" the driver asked.

"Cape Town."

"Sorry, I'm only going as far as Humansdorp, but get in. I'll take you that far."

Humansdorp was only about sixty miles away. I got in the back seat, half dazed by the vision, but wondering why the driver was taking me only sixty miles. According to the vision, that Pontiac was to take me all the way to Cape Town.

A dignified man sat in the back seat beside me. As soon as I got in, he looked at me and said, "I *know* you."

"No, you don't know me."

"Yes, I do. You've got a brother Harold, haven't you?"

103

"Why, yes, I do."

"Where is he?"

"Australia. He's an artist."

"How's your sister, Ethel—and your brother Cecil—and your sister, Rene?"

"They're all okay. How do you know them?"

"Why, I was born in Oudtshoorn. I went to school with the Thom family. Which one are you?"

"I'm the youngest—Robert."

He laughed and laughed. "Isn't this something?" he exclaimed. "And now here you are in the Navy! Where'd you say you were going?"

"Cape Town."

"All right, then, to Cape Town we'll go!"

"But that's a long way out of your way. . . ."

"Poof! It's the least we can do for an old friend." So, that night, I was in Cape Town.

It didn't take me long to get over to Ken Sawyer's house. He and his wife, Peggy, were glad to see me. I explained to them how God had been dealing with me about a ministry, and how I felt led to come to their home for a few days of prayer and fasting.

"Brother Tommy," Ken said warmly, "the house is yours; you can pray as long as you like."

"Goodness! You're probably famished after such a long day's travel!" Peggy spoke up. "What can I get for you?"

"Just a cup of warm water."

"Oh, you're beginning your fast already?"

"Yes," I replied. "It's important." (I didn't tell them that I was already in the eighth day of the fast.)

The days of prayer that followed were very precious to me. I felt myself becoming more and more sensitive to the will of God. Hour after hour was spent on my knees in praise and worship. I almost felt like I was in another world.

But on the eleventh evening of my fast, I became very hungry. Ken and Peggy were in the living room, and I was sitting at the dining room table doing a little reading. Suddenly, terrible stomach cramps took hold of me. I bent over the table and held my stomach, hoping the cramps would go away in a few seconds. But no sooner did one cramp subside than another one began. Peggy would have fixed me some broth, I knew, but I was sure that God had told me I was to fast for two weeks, and I didn't want to disobey.

"Oh, God, you've *got* to feed me!" I prayed under my breath. "You've got to feed me *now!*"

No sooner had I prayed that prayer than my spiritual "eyes" were opened and I saw a tall angel standing before me holding a large cornucopia full of fruit. At first I thought I was suffering a hallucination. I closed my eyes, leaned against the back of the chair and tried to relax. But when I opened my eyes, the angel was still there.

Perhaps it was a vision. I'm rather inclined to think so, considering the nature of what took place between that angel and myself. Not a word was spoken between us, but instinctively, I "knew" that the fruit in that horn of plenty was for me, and that all I had to do was open my mouth and I would be fed. So I tilted my head back and opened my mouth wide.

Immediately, the angel came over beside me, and began to shake the fruit out of the cornucopia into my mouth. He shook and shook, and there was no chewing necessary. I felt this "fruit" melting in my mouth and flowing down my throat. It was sweet and juicy. When the angel had shaken all the fruit out of the cornucopia, he turned, took two or three steps toward the kitchen, and suddenly disappeared.

For a moment I sat there in a daze. Then it began to dawn on me how good I really felt. Every cramp was gone. I felt like I had just had a seven-course meal! Such a tremendous sense of well-being enveloped me that I began to laugh in the Spirit. I laughed so hard, I couldn't sit there any longer. Slipping off the chair, I relaxed on the floor under the table and laughed and laughed and laughed, while tears of hilarity ran out the corners of my eyes and trickled down the sides of my face.

By that time, Ken and Peggy had heard the commotion, and were standing in the doorway of the dining room, staring at me in amazement.

"Brother Tommy's really getting blessed!" Ken said.

"Mercy!" Peggy replied. "Is it catching?"

"I hope so," Ken replied.

Still laughing, I crawled out from under the table and walked out to the kitchen, staggering like I was intoxicated. I was drunk in the Spirit.

"Praise the Lord, Tommy!" Ken shouted.

About that time another wave of glory hit me. I sat down at the kitchen table and laughed so hard I could hardly get my breath. Again, unable to hold myself on the chair, I slipped to the floor, laughing and praying in tongues.

When I finally quieted down later that evening, I had no more pain, and no more weakness. I knew I could finish my fast now.

By the time the fourteenth day arrived, I knew why God had told me to come to Cape Town. The power of God's Spirit was now upon me in a new way. Through those repeated times of prayer, God had revealed that He was calling me to the under-privileged people of the Cape, and I was now ready to begin working toward that ministry.

"Dear God," I said, "if you can use this sailor, then I'm Yours for the rest of my life."

CHAPTER NINE

"BUT GOD TOLD ME, SIR!"

When I got back home to Joyce and the kids in Pretoria, I could hardly wait to share the good news with them.

"We're going back to Cape Town," I announced. "God's got a ministry for me among the poor people there."

A cheer went up from the kids, and Joyce began to cry. "You're really serious about the ministry, aren't you?" she said tearfully. "Oh, Bob, I'm so glad!"

So when I got back on base, I went to see my senior officer, Commander Johnson (who is now the Admiral of the fleet), about getting a transfer out of the Navy to the Army base at Cape Town. Not having any formal training for the ministry, I didn't think I was ready to leave the Armed Forces altogether; but if I could just get down to the Cape, this would be a step in the right direction. I had no particular reason for transferring from the Navy to the Army, except for the vague feeling that a change would be good for me.

It was October 22, 1948. As I expected, the Commander refused permission for the transfer, but said that the final decision would rest with the Naval Headquarters at Durban. He said he'd let me know when he received word. In the meantime, I had plenty of time to fast and pray about my forthcoming move.

One of the big problems, I knew, would be to find a home for my family. Almost every empty house down on the Cape had been commandeered by the government in order to provide housing for the thousands upon thousands of married servicemen stationed in that area. But even so, there simply weren't enough houses to go around, and the Government Housing Office had long waiting lists. And even when you *did* get a house, it was never one of your own choosing. You simply took what was available and that was that.

So I realized what an unlikely thing I was asking when I began to pray for a house at Seapoint in Cape Town. "Lord," I said, "it looks almost impossible in the natural!" But I remembered how the Lord had said, "What things soever ye desire, when ye pray, *believe that ye receive them*, and ye shall have them" (Mark 11:24). So, in accordance with all that God had been teaching me about faith, I began to thank Him for a home.

Finally, through some friends in Cape Town, I learned of a nice house that was available at 14 Burnham Road in Seapoint. "*This is it*," God seemed to say. "*This house is yours if you will claim it in Jesus' name!*"

So I knew I must become very definite in my faith and begin to praise God for *that* house—as well as the necessary permission from Naval Headquarters to transfer to the Army.

For a month, I waited on some word about my transfer, but no word came. So, on November twenty-second, at two in the afternoon, I went into the office of Lieutenant Quixley, my superior officer.

"Sir," I said, "I want to know about the application I made for transfer to the Army."

"It was turned down," he said flatly.

"But, sir," I said, "God told me I'd be going to Cape Town and that I'd be on the train on December twenty-second."

"*Who* told you?"

"God, sir."

"What the h_____!" he snorted. "That will be the day when the South African Navy takes orders from God!"

As soon as I heard that, I returned to my office, picked up the telephone and dialed the South African Railways.

"This is Petty Officer Robert Thom, South African Navy," I said in a loud voice. "Please book me, Mrs. Thom and five children to leave on your eight p.m. train on the twenty-second of December for Cape Town."

Then I phoned three different moving companies to get bids on moving my furniture. The lowest bid was from the Norman Spencer Moving Company, so I instructed them to ship my furniture on December twenty-second, at government expense, to 40 Arthurs Road, Seapoint, Cape Town, which was the address of the Apostolic Faith Mission where our family had formerly gone to church. (Pastor Crompton had previously told me that they could give me temporary storage anytime I needed it.)

As soon as I completed my calls, Lieutenant Quixley was in my doorway! "Thom, you're under arrest for insubordination," he barked out. "You've got no right to book a seat on that train!"

110

"But God told me, sir. . . ."

"I don't give a d_____ *what* God told you! Your transfer is not approved, and you've got no right to do this!"

"All right," I said. "If that's the way it is, then that's the way it will be." So I dropped the matter for the time being.

But about a month later, on the twentieth of December, I again went over to Quixley's office.

"Sir," I said, "today is Monday, and the day after tomorrow I'll be catching the train for Cape Town."

"Listen, Thom," he replied, trying to control his temper, "I thought we had that problem settled. Didn't you cancel those reservations?"

"No, sir, God wouldn't let me."

"D_____ you, Thom!" he yelled. "What the h_____ kind of place do you think we're running here? You're under arrest for insubordination!"

I knew he meant business this time. He promptly marched me down to General Headquarters to Commander Johnson's office, and stated his case against me.

"All right, Thom," the Commander said quietly, "the Lieutenant is right. You're under arrest for insubordination and disobedience to your superior officer."

"I didn't mean to be insubordinate, sir."

"Then how do you know that you're going to Cape Town? And how do you know that you're getting a transfer?"

"The Lord God told me, sir. I've been fasting and praying, and God told me I would leave—and I *am* leaving on that train."

He looked at me in amazement. "Thom," he went on, "even if you get the transfer into the

Army, how can you be sure they'll move you to Cape Town?"

"*God* told me, sir."

He just sat there shaking his head. Then, in a defeated tone of voice, he said, "Lieutenant, pick up that phone and ring the base in Durban—and have someone see what happened to this man's application for transfer to the Army. If it's been granted, tell them to ring us back."

So I sat there in the Commander's office, waiting and praying. At twenty minutes after four, the phone rang. I could tell by the angry way the Commander was talking that my transfer had been granted. After a short argument, the Commander slammed down the receiver. "Get the h_____ out of here, Thom!" he shouted. "You can thank your lucky stars, you've got your d_____ transfer!"

"Not my lucky stars, sir," I replied, "but I thank my Lord and Savior, Jesus Christ!"

On the morning of the twenty-second (the day we were scheduled to leave for Cape Town), I went over to the Army Depot to get my orders. I had to fill out a number of forms, and finally found myself in the office of one of the commanding officers. "We are transferring you down to a camp in the Cape," he began. My fingers began to tingle with excitement.

"However," he went on, "due to the vacation time and the Christmas holidays, we can't get you on the train for thirty days, so you'll have to stay here in camp."

"But, sir," I said, "what if I had reservations?"

"Then you could leave tonight."

"Then here they are, sir," I said, pulling the reservations out of my pocket.

He looked them over for a few seconds, then said, "Where are your wife and children?"

"Well, I suppose by now the taxi cab has taken them to Pretoria Station, where they'll be waiting for their tickets."

"But it's not as easy as that," the officer said. "What about your furniture? You've got to have three bids, and it's got to be moved at government expense."

"I know," I replied, smiling. "I took care of all that when I was in the Navy." And I pulled out more papers to show him that all arrangements for moving had been completed. "In fact," I went on, "the Norman Spencer Moving Company moved my furniture out at eight this morning. It's now on the train, heading for Cape Town."

The officer was more than a little astonished. "Things just aren't this simple in the Army," he quipped. "There's got to be something wrong somewhere."

But everything was all right. So they signed me up and issued my uniform, and within thirty-five minutes, I was officially transferred to the South African Army.

That evening at eight o'clock our whole family boarded the train for Cape Town, and arrived two days later on the morning of Thursday, December twenty-fourth. Before leaving our seats, we all bowed our heads and praised God for the house at 14 Burnham Road.

Ken and Peggy Sawyer were at the station to greet us, and they took us to their home for the Christmas holidays. On the day after Christmas, which was Saturday, I went over to the Government Housing Office and put in my application for a house. I was told that it was impossible—that there were thousands on the waiting list before me. Besides, on Wednesday, December thirtieth, the Government Housing Act would come to an end, and there would be no more housing available through that agency. It was bad news. I knew I couldn't afford to buy a house, and the housing control seemed my only hope.

Nevertheless, I refused to be discouraged. God had promised us a house, hadn't He? I was sure I could depend on His word. So, on Sunday, December twenty-seventh, we all went to the Mission together, and I testified that God was going to give us a house.

By Wednesday, December thirtieth, I still hadn't heard anything from the Government Housing Office. At five p.m. that day, that office would be closed forever. We prayed and prayed throughout the day, but five o'clock came and went, and nothing happened. But we were still hanging on.

When the evening paper came, I read with a great deal of interest a news item about the closing of the Housing Control Office. It said that the last official act of the office was to commandeer a house under the Government Act, and give it to a soldier in the standing army. A letter had been sent out to this soldier at five minutes until five, the article said. The name of the soldier was not given, so it was a glimmer of hope.

Two days later, when I opened the mail, there was the letter! We had a house—at 14 Burnham Road, Seapoint, Capetown, within walking distance of the Mission, and 200 yards from the house where I had been saved.

"PRAISE THE LORD!" I shouted. Joyce, Ken and Peggy came running, along with the kids. "What's happened?" they chorused.

"We've got a house!" I announced.

"Wonderful! Praise the Lord! Hallelujah!" they all cried.

Young Drummond looked at us all somewhat puzzled. "Why is everybody so surprised?" he asked innocently. "God always keeps His promises, doesn't He?"

CHAPTER TEN

GOING ON GOD'S PAYROLL

In spite of the rapid succession of events in 1948, everything seemed to come to a standstill during the next two or three years—that is, so far as my call to the ministry was concerned. It was a difficult time for me; I couldn't understand what God was waiting for. Was I too immature? Did I need training? Or could I be mistaken about this "call" to God's work?

The work at the Army base was going well. I was Quartermaster in an Engineering Unit, and had charge of the entire payroll. In addition, I was responsible for all quarters' stores, which handled millions of dollars' worth of materiels every year. It was a huge task to assign the troops to our 300 or more buildings, and keep the men supplied with clothing and equipment. But I enjoyed the challenge of doing a big job.

Still, the job at the base could never take the place of a full-time ministry for Jesus Christ. So, with some degree of discouragement, I kept praying for God to show me what to do.

Another thing that was beginning to depress me was Joyce's growing skepticism about the baptism in the Spirit. I hadn't been aware of this problem until we moved to Seapoint. Ever since her conversion, Joyce had been an enthusiastic Christian; and though I received the baptism before she did, I had been confident she would receive this deeper experience soon. But after we'd been attending the Mission for a while, her doubts began to show.

"You know," she said to me one day, "God forgive me if I'm wrong, but it's just hard to accept some of the things they preach down at that Mission."

"Oh?" I said, a little surprised. "What do you mean?"

"Well, this healing business, for one thing. I don't mean to be a skeptic, Bob—you know I love the Lord—but if God still performs miracles today, then why aren't *you* healed?"

"I don't know," I replied, "but God *does* heal today. Remember what I told you about Hope Anderson, and how God healed her of dystrophy?"

"Yes, that was great—but why hasn't it worked for you?"

"I don't know—God must have His reasons."

"Yes, that's what they say down at the Mission."

"But what else *can* they say?"

"They could be honest and admit that maybe they've been wrong about healing—and a few other things."

"Other things? Such as?"

"Such as all this talk about the baptism in the Spirit."

"But, Joyce, why would you *ever* doubt that?"

"Just because I don't see any evidence of all this *power* they're always talking about," she replied. "They *talk* about having power to witness, but hardly anyone gets saved. They *talk* about having power to heal the sick, but no one gets healed. Bob, it's hard to believe in a power that doesn't work."

117

"But you'll have to admit that the baptism has made a big change in most of them," I reminded her.

"Yes," she said, looking me right in the eye, "that I'll grant you. All the Spirit-baptized now clap their hands and shout hallelujah—but, Bob, that's not the power that *Jesus* talked about!"

Whew! In a way, I knew she was right. I sat there silently, thinking about my own baptism in the Spirit in Brother McQuade's house. As glorious an experience as that was, yet I had to admit that I wasn't altogether satisfied with the power that had been manifested in my life *since* that experience. Something was blocking the *full flow* of the Holy Spirit's power—but I hadn't been able to find the key to this mystery. I went to bed that evening feeling a little discouraged. Little did I know how close I was to finding the answer.

In the fall of 1951, I learned that I was up for promotion on the base. That meant that I would soon have the highest ranking position in our unit. If God wanted me in the ministry, I couldn't understand why He was blessing me with such success in the Army.

About the same time, the people down at the Mission were trying to decide whom to send to the big youth convention up at Maranatha Park Camp Grounds in Johannesburg, 930 miles north. Since I was the Vice Chairman of our youth organization, and since I had a week's vacation in October, on the very week of the convention, they voted twenty-five dollars to send me. According to what Pastor Crompton told me, I was in for a double spiritual treat. The youth convention was to close on Thursday night, and then on Friday, the Bosworth Healing Revival was to begin in the same auditorium.

It would have been a blessing for the whole family to have gone along, but we had six children at that time and it was too expensive. So Joyce agreed to stay at home while I made the trip to Johannesburg.

I had heard a lot about the amazing healing ministry of F. F. Bosworth, author of *Christ the Healer*. Many people said that unbelievable miracles took place in his services—such as the blind receiving their sight, and the deaf receiving their hearing, and the crippled throwing away their crutches. I was eager to see if what I had heard was really true. Who knows—I might even get my asthma healed!

When I arrived at the campgrounds, the Maranatha Park Auditorium was buzzing with excitement. It was a big, corrugated iron building with open sides, which had been especially constructed for religious conventions. The building boasted a seating capacity of over 9,000, counting the seats in the large balcony. What a thrill it was to see Christian teenagers from all over South Africa filling that large tabernacle!

On Thursday night, the chairman of the meeting warned all who were planning to stay the rest of the week for the Bosworth Revival to be sure to come early if we expected good seats. So, early Friday afternoon, I went over to the auditorium and sat down in a seat in the second row from the front. If these healings were real, I wanted to see them at close range. Not that I was there as a doubting Thomas. But after my conversations with Joyce, I *had* to know the truth.

119

"Lord," I said, "either divine healing works or it doesn't work. If it works (and I believe it does), I hope You won't mind my giving Your work a close-up inspection!"

The service wasn't scheduled to begin until the evening. But looking around me, I noticed that I wasn't the *only* one who'd come that early. Actually, several hundred people were already scattered throughout the auditorium, and others were arriving steadily. By the time the service was to begin, every seat was taken and the overflow crowd spilled out on the grass surrounding the open auditorium. The area in front of me, between the seats and the platform, was filled with wheel chairs and cots. The organist was playing some familiar Gospel songs.

The service was opened with all those thousands of people lifting their voices in song. Later on, a short sermon was delivered by the associate evangelist. It was after the evangelist had finished speaking, and we were all praying quietly, that the Holy Spirit began to move over that congregation in great power. I heard people all around me sobbing. The first thing I knew *I* was crying too! The tears rolled down my cheeks and dropped on my shirt. I felt like I was being washed, inside and out, by the power of God. And then God spoke, in that peculiar way I cannot explain, and said to me, "*Robert, this night I have called you to work full time for Me. I have called you to leave all earthly security and to preach My Gospel, to proclaim the message of deliverance, to bring the Gospel to the poor, to heal the sick, to cast out devils.*"

In a flash, I saw what had been hindering my walk in the Spirit. For three years now, God had been waiting on me to make up my mind. Was I going to step out in faith and obedience into full time service for Him, or was I not?

Somehow, I had been thinking that when God wanted me to leave the Army, He would shuffle my circumstances around in such a way that I would be *compelled* to make the move. But now I saw everything in a new light. God wasn't going to *force* me out of the Army; if I left the Army, it would be on my own choosing. God had called. It was up to me to take the step of faith and respond to His call.

I thought about Abram leaving Ur of the Chaldees. God hadn't compelled him to make that move, had He? He simply revealed His will, and it was up to Abram to decide whether or not he would take that drastic step of faith and leave Ur.

When I saw this, I realized with some embarrassment that this was the same lesson God had taught me many times before. He wanted me to walk in faith. But He wasn't going to do the walking for me. If I would walk, He would make the way before me. But if I insisted on standing still, nothing would happen.

I wept and wept. I knew the time of decision had come.

"Lord," I said, "my wife is a thousand miles from here. She doesn't understand these things. She doesn't understand the baptism of the Spirit. But if this is Your voice speaking to me, I'm willing to be obedient. I'll give up my position down at the base and follow You."

I knew what a serious thing that was to say. To leave a good job and step out to serve God with no guarantee of any kind of pay would seem like a crazy thing to do—especially to Joyce. In fact, a decision like this could easily ruin my family, unless God were really in it. And *that*, I had to know for sure. There could be no mistakes.

"Lord," I said again, "I've got to know that this is really Your voice speaking to me, and not some notion of my own. So, as a sign to me, I ask You to baptize Joyce in the Holy Spirit very soon—and let it be on a Friday afternoon. Then I will know that You have spoken."

I knew how easily people can be deceived on matters of guidance. And surely God wouldn't mind if I did a little double checking. After all, I had seen too many people running off after shadows and making some bad mistakes.

About that time, the seventy-four-year-old Bosworth got up and began to speak. He was a tall, dignified man who had ministered to millions. For a few minutes, he told that crowd of 10,000 about the power of Jesus.

"Now," he continued, "there are nine people here who've had mastoid operations. Some of you are partially deaf, others of you are totally deaf. Where are you? Stand to your feet if you hear me. Or, if anyone here is sitting next to a deaf person, bring him to the front."

Soon there were nine deaf or partially deaf people standing at the front of that great auditorium. Bosworth came down and laid his hands on them one by one.

"Thou deaf demon, come out of this woman in the name of Jesus!" he commanded. Instantly, the woman looked up in amazement and said, "I can hear! I can hear!" The audience gasped. Every one of those people received their hearing. In each case, Bosworth took time to test the results after prayer, so that all present could see what had happened.

122

And this was done throughout the evening, as many other miracles took place. By the time that service was over, I knew beyond any doubt that God *does* perform miracles of healing today.

By the next evening, I felt like I could trust God for anything! When it came time to pray for the sick, I sat there in my seat, praying along with the evangelist. Suddenly, there was a commotion in front of me.

"What's going on here?" I asked myself, looking up quickly. There I saw two women with broken backs who had been brought to the meeting on cots. They both jumped up and began praising God, hugging each other and dancing for joy! Another fellow with an iron brace and a built-up shoe removed his brace and saw his leg grow out 2½ inches! By that time, people were beginning to scream and shout all over that auditorium. Some with stiff legs began to walk up and down the aisles. Some who had not been able to see were exclaiming, "I can see! I can see!" Everybody was crying. Such a wave of the healing power of God I had never seen. *None* of us had. Soon people began getting up out of their seats and going forward to pray. Before that service was over, almost two thousand people had been saved.

On Saturday night there were many more miracles. But, to me, the most exciting thing about that service was the announcement that Bosworth would be in Cape Town on the following weekend. "Praise the Lord!" I said under my breath. "I'll take Joyce! If *this* doesn't convince her, *nothing* will."

Before leaving that auditorium that evening, I elbowed my way through the crowd, hoping to shake hands with Bosworth. But it seemed that everyone else had that idea too, and I had to wait in a long line.

"This is probably a waste of energy," I thought. "There won't be time for anything more than a 'God bless you.'"

But when I finally stood in front of Bosworth, he clasped my hand warmly like I was an old friend and began to ask me all about myself. When I told him that God had called me to a ministry among the poor people of the Cape, he showed great interest.

"Brother, you ought to come to America sometime," he said. "We could do some exciting things together."

"I'd sure like that," I replied, somewhat taken aback by his suggestion.

"And I too," he said. "I love to help young men get started in the ministry. That's every bit as important to me as the large crusades."

"Brother Bosworth, you can count on it," I replied. "One of these days I'll come to America to visit you."

"Good!" he said, smiling. "I'd love to help train another 'Timothy!'"

"Imagine that!" I said within myself as I walked away from Bosworth. "He actually wants to help *me!*"

I traveled back to Cape Town, more certain than ever that God had called me to His work. When I got back home, I burst in the door and began to tell Joyce all about the things I'd seen and the short talk I'd had with Bosworth. "You've got to see what I saw," I blurted out. "This fellow Bosworth is the greatest I've ever seen—and he's coming to Cape-town this weekend. Will you go?"

"Did you get your asthma healed?" she asked.

"Well, no, but a lot of other people got healed."

"I just can't understand that. Everybody gets healed but you."

"But I *will* get healed," I replied. "If He's done it for others, He'll do it for me too."

"Maybe."

But when Bosworth came to town, she agreed to go. I think she was curious to see what had me so excited. So she got all the kids ready, and off we went to the service. The power of God fell just like it had at Johannesburg. Joyce was very interested. When we got home that evening, I said to her, "Well, what do you think?"

Tears welled up in her eyes. "It was beautiful," she said. "Just beautiful!" But all too quickly the campaign came to an end, and Bosworth moved on. "Joyce," I said, "I have the feeling that this is just the beginning of what God wants to do in this city."

"Yes," she responded. "I wonder if he'll ever come back."

"I don't know," I said, "but even if he doesn't, the work of God must still go on."

"Yes, but how?"

"I'm going to write some letters—to T. L. Osborne—or Oral Roberts—or maybe Billy Graham. I'll invite them to come and have campaigns here in Cape Town."

So that's what I did. But all of them wrote back and said they were solidly booked up for a long time in advance. Then one Wednesday God spoke to me. "*Go out yourself*," He said in gentle reproof. "*Haven't I called you to preach My Gospel?*"

"Lord, forgive me," I said. "I'll do it—but I'm

not quitting my job at the base until You baptize Joyce in the Spirit. We've got a deal, remember?"

But I knew I had to obey God if I wanted to have fellowship with Him. So, that night I hitched a small generator to the back of a borrowed truck, drove out into the poor district, and started an open-air revival. They didn't have electricity in that area, so the electric lights were an attraction in themselves. A little girl nine years of age was brought into the meeting, deaf and dumb. In the name of the Lord Jesus Christ, I cast out the dumb spirit.

When the lights had been dimmed, and we were getting ready to leave, I saw a man with his wife and five daughters all dressed in white, running across the field. The man was very excited.

"Sir," he said, "I am the father of the little deaf and dumb girl whom you prayed for tonight. We are Hindus. My little girl is nine years of age, and I have never heard her speak until tonight. I understand that you prayed for her in the name of your God, the Lord Jesus Christ." That man, his wife, and five daughters knelt down and accepted Jesus as their personal Savior.

The revival got bigger and bigger until within three weeks, we had as many as 15,000 standing on the open field. One night, about 5,000 people accepted Jesus as their Savior.

On another night, one of the senior lecturers of the University of South Africa in Pretoria happened to be passing by. His name was Mr. Tromp. He had come to Cape Town for a few days of vacation at the seashore. Being a Christian man, he was greatly interested in the large crowd of people he saw listening to the Word of God.

As he stood there on the edge of the crowd (he told us later), he heard me say there was a man with a hernia standing there in the audience whom God wanted to heal. He knew he was that man, although he said nobody knew about his affliction except him and God. For nineteen months he had been praying that God would heal him. The minute I made that statement, he raised his hand to acknowledge his condition, and in the name of Jesus Christ I commanded the affliction to leave him. Instantly, the hernia disappeared!

During those days I read every book I could find on faith. I read the life stories of Smith Wigglesworth, Charles Finney and John Wesley. The impression became deeper and deeper that God wanted me in His service full time.

It was three weeks after the Bosworth Revival at Johannesburg that God manifested Himself to me in a special way. I went off to work that Friday morning as usual. About four p.m. the telephone rang. It was a Sister Maude Solomon, a friend of Gladys Webster's.

"Brother Thom," she said, "is that you?"

"Yes," I said. "What's all that noise going on in the background?"

"Oh," she laughed, "I'm glad you can hear that!"

"Well, what is it?"

"That's your wife speaking in tongues. The Lord just baptized her with the Holy Ghost!"

"You're joking!"

"No! It's true! Just listen." She stopped talking long enough for me to hear Joyce's voice clearly. Sure enough, she was praying in some unknown language.

"Praise God!" I said. "This is *exactly* what I prayed for."

"It is?"

"Yes, ma'am! Three weeks ago today, I told God if He wanted me in the ministry full time, He must baptize Joyce in the Holy Ghost soon, and that it must happen on a Friday afternoon!"

"No!" she said in amazement. "You prayed that prayer?"

"Yes, ma'am!"

"And it's happened just as you prayed!"

"Yes, isn't Jesus wonderful?"

I hung up the phone, and sat there for a moment in a daze. "Lord," I said, after awhile, "You don't need to say anymore. I'll obey You." I promptly went over to the Commander's office. (He happened to be my brother-in-law.)

"Major," I announced, "I'm applying for my discharge papers. I want to leave on the thirty-first of December."

"You're quitting? Why?"

"I'm going into the ministry."

"You d____ fool! You'd better think this over. Don't you realize I've got you up for promotion? You'll soon be the top man in your unit!"

"I know, but God told me to get out."

"You expect me to believe that? Why, in the name of common sense, would God ever tell you to do an idiotic thing like that?"

"I don't know," I replied with a grin. "He must have something in mind."

He shook his head incredulously. "You've really gone nuts over this religion business, haven't you?" he sneered. "Pretty soon you'll have Joyce as crazy as you are."

"I guess she already is," I replied. "She just got filled with the Holy Ghost this afternoon."

He turned in disgust to walk out of his office. "Okay," he said, "if you want to bow out, that's your dumb mistake. Just don't come crying on *my* shoulder when you're starving."

When I got home that evening, Joyce threw her arms around me and wept for joy at her new-found experience in the Spirit. "Oh, Bob, it's so wonderful!" she sobbed. "I feel like I've stepped into a whole new life!"

"Yes, it *will* be," I said, laughing, "—in more ways than you think."

"What do you mean," she said, drawing back and looking at me through tear-filled eyes.

"I'm going into the ministry full-time."

"You're quitting your job at the base?"

"Yes. I can buy my way out for fifty-two British pounds."

For a moment she became dead serious. "What will we live on?"

"Honey," I said, "the God Who calls will also provide."

She started to laugh. "Wheeee!" she squealed. "We're going on God's payroll!"

We both stood there for the longest time laughing and crying.

During the next few days, we prayed earnestly for the needed money. In fact, we decided to ask for a total of sixty-three pounds: fifty-two pounds to buy my way out of the Army, and eleven pounds for a few days' vacation. Of course, with my asthma, I could have easily gotten a hundred percent pension, but I felt sure God was going to heal me; so I decided it would be better to buy my way out.

One evening, I went to a prayer meeting. I had decided I needed to pray very earnestly for the sixty-three pounds that evening. When I got home, there was a man talking to Joyce at the gate.

"Brother Thom," he said, "your wife's got a check for you."

"Yes," I said. "Sixty-three pounds."

He looked at me with surprise. "How do you know? Did your wife call you or something?"

"How could I have phoned him?" Joyce interrupted. "You just handed me the check over the gate a few minutes ago, and I've been standing here talking to you since."

"Yes, of course," he said, turning to me, "but how did you know?"

"Well," I replied, "I just prayed for sixty-three pounds. And when I pray, I expect God to answer."

He was startled. "It's a miracle!" he said. "Wait'll I tell my wife about *this!*"

CHAPTER ELEVEN

WHO NEEDS FOUR PILLOWS?

By the time the last of December rolled around, everyone in my unit knew I was leaving. The Major still thought I was making a bad mistake. I had a good record of performance, as evidenced by my seven medals and decorations. Nevertheless, God had made His will clear, and I knew there was nothing else for me to do but obey.

So on December thirty-first, I was given a military farewell. The Commanding Officer and all the men of the unit met in a hall to give me a grand send-off. When I walked in, every man stood at attention as I was escorted to the head table.

The liquor was brought out, and everyone began to fill their glasses. Some of the fellows grinned and winked at one another; they knew how I felt about drinking.

"Make mine ginger ale," I said loud enough for them all to hear. "I want to leave the Army in full possession of my faculties." They all laughed.

After the Commanding Officer made his speech about me, mentioning all the things I'd done for the Army, they all had their toasts ready. But first, I had to give my answering speech. Not feeling right about toasting with them and their liquor, I replied this way:

"Officer Commanding, Officers, Warrant Officers, NCO's and men: I appreciate this wonderful gesture of farewell this afternoon. I'm deeply touched by it. But ever since Christ came into my life, I have had a real change of heart. I've come to abhor the liquor that disrupted my home and ruined my life and nearly sent me to a suicide's grave. I would appreciate it this afternoon if, before you lift those glasses to toast me, you would just bow your heads in prayer and allow me to thank God for my years in the service, and pray God's blessing over you as my comrades."

They put their glasses down, and I prayed. God's anointing came upon me, and by the time I said "amen," there was some real struggling going on amongst those men to hold back tears. Before they had a chance to offer their toasts, I put on my cap, marched up to the Officer Commanding and saluted in dead silence. Then, turning on my heel, I marched out of that hall into a new life, amidst the thunderous applause of the men.

At one minute past twelve that night, I was officially out of the Army.

Nobody will ever know how free I felt when I woke up on New Year's Day, 1952! There was nothing more to hold me back; all earthly security was left behind; I was now committed to a life of naked faith in the promises of God.

"But don't let me be worried about material things, Lord," I prayed. "Let me be concerned only about the millions and millions of people who haven't yet heard the Gospel. Fill me with love for the lost, and let me understand how terrible it is to go into eternity without Christ. That's the important thing. You'll take care of us and our material needs if we keep You and Your work first."

Bouncing out of bed, I began to hum a good old Gospel tune as I dressed. But I had only hummed through a couple lines when I began to cough. I coughed so hard I had to sit down on the edge of the bed to catch my breath.

"This miserable asthma!" I growled to myself. "It's going to be the death of me someday!" Then I went into a coughing spasm that lasted for perhaps fifteen minutes. When it finally subsided, I felt weak and exhausted.

"You and your stupid dreams of a ministry to the poor people!" the devil suggested. "Who wants to listen to a wheezing machine like you?" I rebuked him weakly, and said something about serving Jesus even if I died in the process.

And that was altogether possible. My condition had advanced to the stage where I was practically living on ephedrine tablets and I couldn't lie down to sleep. I always propped myself up on four pillows.

On the third day of January, I took Joyce and the kids to a church convention up in the nearby mountains. I felt like this would be a good opportunity to get away for a weekend of spiritual refreshment before beginning my ministry among the people of the Cape.

But everything went wrong. We stayed in a little log cabin, and Joyce was going to do the cooking on a portable gas stove. On the first day, she was boiling some water, and when she went to pour this water, she spilled it on her legs and burned herself severely. I treated the burn with whatever first aid I could find there in the cabin, and told Joyce she'd better lie down for a while. That meant that I had to watch the kids and cook the evening meal. That night, neither of us got much sleep. Joyce spent most of the night in pain, and I spent most of the night coughing and trying to get my breath.

When we got back home late Sunday evening, I made up my mind that something had to be done about my condition. "Lord," I prayed before retiring that night, "how can I go on like this? Here You've called me to preach the Gospel and minister to the sick, but how can I do it when I'm sick myself? You've got to *do* something!"

"*No*," the Lord seemed to say, "*YOU'VE got to do something*."

"*Me* do something? But *what?*"

"*Put your faith into action*."

Just then another attack came on, and I coughed so long and hard I thought I'd die. Joyce came in and fanned me, but it didn't help. Then she opened the window, thinking some fresh air would do some good. But there was nothing else to do but suffer it out. When I finally began to quiet down some, I began to think about what God had said to me. "*Put your faith into action*."

Strange that God should say that—*again!* He knew how earnestly I believed the great teachings of His Word about His healing power. I not only believed it but preached it. I thought about Psalm 103:3 where David speaks of God as the One "who healeth all thy diseases." I remembered how Isaiah foretold the crucifixion of Jesus, saying, "With his stripes we are healed" (Isaiah 53:5). I *really believed* those statements. But God seemed to be saying that I had to *prove* my faith by doing something.

"All right," I said aloud. "If it's action You want, then here goes."

I got up from my knees, gathered up three of the four pillows I always used to prop myself up with, and put them in the closet. "From now on," I said to Joyce, "I'm going to sleep like any other normal person! If God wants to heal me, then I don't need four pillows to keep me alive!"

"Are you sure?" Joyce asked doubtfully.

"Yes. And the pills will go too," I replied, picking up the bottle of ephedrine tablets and walking out to the kitchen. I turned on the faucet and dumped them all down the sink. "It will be kill or cure," I said, "but I'm going to stand on God's Word." I went back to bed and lay flat on my back for the first time in months.

About half an hour later, I began coughing again. It felt like all my air was cut off. My chest heaved and I struggled to get a breath. Suddenly everything went black and I passed out.

In that unconscious state, something strange happened. I'm not sure whether it was a dream or a vision, but I felt myself falling down into the bowels of the earth. Was it an abandoned mine shaft, or some dark mysterious pit? I wasn't sure, but it was musty and damp down there.

When I hit the bottom, I seemed to be in a gloomy, underground cavern. Looking out ahead of me, I could make out a wide, murky lake. I walked to the lake's edge and there I saw snakes and rats. Frogs were jumping around, and there were scorpions and spiders.

"Where am I?" I whispered to myself. Then, looking far across the lake, I saw what appeared to be a boat with one man in it rowing slowly but surely toward me. Instantly I knew it was the

Angel of Death coming for me. I wanted to turn and run, but my feet were glued to the spot.

When my eyes became more accustomed to the shadows, I saw there were millions and millions of people in that lake. I especially noticed the heads of the women floating below the surface, their hair loose and swirling.

"You asked Me for a vision of the lost," a Voice said. *"Each hair on these millions of heads represents a lost soul in eternity. See how many millions there are!"*

As I looked out over that vast lake and saw the many, many people there, I fell to my knees and began to weep, not for myself, but for the millions of lost souls I saw. "Oh, God," I cried, "don't let me die yet! Let me go back to the land of the living, that I might work for You and bring the lost to Christ. Somebody must help them! Let me go back! Let me go back!"

Then I began to recite the twenty-third Psalm. *"The Lord is my shepherd; I shall not want. . . ."*

As I tried to say those words, my breathing became more and more difficult. I grew dizzy and fell backwards, still whispering the words of that Psalm. Finally I came to those words, *"Yea, though I walk through the valley of the shadow of death, I will fear no evil: for thou art with me; thy rod and thy staff they comfort me."*

Just then I felt a pair of unseen hands slipping underneath my body and lifting me out of that pit. I finished the Psalm and started over. Those unseen hands lifted me all the way out, and gently deposited me on a grassy slope alongside a brook. Just then I was saying, *"He maketh me to lie down in green pastures; He leadeth me beside the still waters. . . ."*

Suddenly I came back to consciousness. It was late at night. I heard somebody praying quietly beside my bed. It was Pastor Crompton. He was saying, "Thank You, Jesus! Thank You, Lord!"

I touched him on the shoulder. "How long have *you* been here?"

He was a little surprised. "Two and a half hours," he grinned. "Are you all right?"

Then it was that I noticed how easily I was breathing. There was no wheezing. No straining. Come to think of it, even my voice sounded different.

"Praise the Lord!" I shouted, just to hear my own voice again. Sure enough, the raspiness was gone. I jumped out of bed and hugged Pastor Crompton and Joyce. "God's healed me!" I shouted. "Can you beat that? I'm healed! My asthma is *gone!*"

Pretty soon all the kids were up. "What's going on?" Drummond asked sleepily.

"Daddy's healed!" Joyce shouted. "Look how easily he's breathing!" They all crowded around and looked at me in wonder.

"Oh, boy," David said, "now I can have my pillow back!" We all laughed and rejoiced for a long time. But finally the pastor left, and we sent the kids back to bed. For the first time in months, I slept like a baby.

The next day, I got up feeling like I owned the world. It was great to be alive. My first thoughts were about the ministry. Seemingly, God had removed the last great barrier, so I decided it was now time to get started in my work.

I went down to see Pastor Crompton. "Pastor," I began, "you know I've cut myself loose for God's work. I'd like to apply to become a minister under the Apostolic Faith Mission."

"Ah, Brother Tommy," the pastor replied, "I'm so glad to hear you say that!" Pulling open a drawer, he produced an application form. "Fill this out, and we'll send it in to church headquarters."

I pulled up a chair, and filled out the long application. All the time I was writing, Pastor Crompton kept saying quietly, "Praise the Lord! Thank You, Jesus!"

When I finished, the pastor said he'd mail it off right away, and I would probably hear from headquarters in a few days. I went home, confident that all would be well.

In a few days, however, I received a letter of rejection. The letter explained that it was contrary to church policy to accept anyone for a missionary assignment who had more than five children. I had six.

"Lord, what do I do now?" I asked in disappointment.

"*Haven't I already told you?*" the Lord seemed to reply.

"Already told me?" I asked in puzzlement. "When? Where?"

Then God brought to my mind a service I had been in several months before where two or three people had prophesied that I would never join any organization and that God would give me a unique ministry whereby I would take the Gospel not only to the Cape, but to many nations.

"Lord, was that really You speaking?" I asked.

"*I have permitted the rejection of your application, that you might see My plan more clearly,*" He seemed to say. "*Do not all things work together for good to them who love Me, for those who are the called according to My purpose?*"

So a few days later after much prayer, I decided to launch out by faith, preaching and teaching wherever God would give me a place. I didn't know it then, but this was the decision which was to launch me into a life more exciting than any I dared dream possible.

CHAPTER TWELVE

FAREWELL TO BEDS AND BRACES

One of my first meetings was held in a home at 19 Bromwell Street in Woodstock, a suburb of Cape Town. I found that home meetings were a good way to minister to the needs of the people, and many were saved and healed.

Aside from the crowd that gathered in the living room that night, there was a daughter in the family who was bedridden.

"What's her problem?" I asked the parents.

"She's got a broken back."

"Oh? What happened?"

"She was injured at the factory. She draws unemployment pay, and gets a little from the union. But it'll be a long time before she'll be able to get out of that bed."

"That's too bad," I said. "Would you like me to pray for her?"

"Oh, yes!" they replied. "Please do!"

So, near the close of the service, I went over to the raised hospital bed where she was lying and prayed a simple prayer for her healing. However, nothing happened that I could see, so I encouraged both her and the parents to have faith, and left the house about nine-thirty.

At five minutes past eleven, my telephone rang.

"Hello. Brother Boetie here," an excited voice said.

"Yes, Brother Boetie," I replied. "Is anything wrong?" Brother Boetie was one of the men who had attended the meeting.

"I thought you would want to know about this," he said. "After you left the meeting tonight, their pastor stopped by and told those people that you are of the devil, and that they must never let you in their house again."

"And what did *they* say?" I replied.

"They told him that you prayed for their daughter. And he said, 'Well, she didn't get healed, did she?' And they said, 'No.' So he said, 'You see, that *proves* he is of the devil; otherwise God would answer his prayers.'"

"And then what happened?"

"Ah, that's the *great* part," he said. "When he said that, that girl jumped out of her bed—and you remember how high it was—she jumped out of that bed and walked right in front of that minister, and she hasn't been on her feet for nineteen months!"

I started to laugh. "Praise God! Isn't that just like the Lord? What did the minister say?"

"Oh, Brother Thom, he was in a terrible state. He just stared at that girl in unbelief, and then he got up and said to us, 'Oh, forgive me, forgive me!' She just kept walking in front of him, and then she even walked down the stairs to the first-floor bathroom!"

After I had hung up the receiver, I laughed and laughed. Then I went and told Joyce and we praised God together.

The next morning, there was a knock on the

door. When I answered, there was a man who introduced himself as the pastor of the family down on Bromwell Street. "Oh, Brother," he said, "please forgive me! I'm so embarrassed!"

"Why, what's wrong?" I said, acting as though I knew nothing about it. Then he told me the whole story and tearfully asked my forgiveness.

"That's all right, it's all forgiven," I said, smiling. "You just didn't understand the healing power of Jesus."

In all my meetings after that, I knew what it must have been like when Jesus was on earth. His presence was so real that it seemed that nothing was impossible.

From that time on, I began to organize witnessing teams to go out and preach and heal the sick. One night my helper and I went out to a place called Elsie's River where we were to have a meeting in the home of a family by the name of Groves. It was a stormy night, and we had to wade through muddy, flooded-out roads to get there. When we arrived, my attention was attracted to a boy about ten years old who was lying on the floor in a full length brace. The brace had a leather section which supported the boy's head and body. There were also iron extensions to which the boy's limbs were strapped.

"Who is he?" I asked one of the men.

"That's Brother and Sister Groves' boy, Collin," the man replied. "He's got a disease of the joints."

During the meeting, I felt moved to pray for him. "Collin," I said, "do you believe in the healing power of Jesus?"

"Yessir."

"And do you believe He can make you well?"

142

"Yessir."

I laid my hands upon him, prayed a brief prayer, and pronounced him well in the name of Jesus.

"Now, then," I said, "do you believe you can walk now?"

"Yessir."

"Would you be willing to have us remove that old brace?"

"Yessir."

So we unstrapped him and helped him to his feet. Immediately he began walking without help, and his face lit up with joy. When the people saw what was happening, they began shouting, "Thank You, Jesus!" And others fell on their knees and began to repent of their sins. No invitation was necessary that night. As soon as they saw this manifestation of God's power, they realized their need of Jesus.

A few days later, I took Peter Dreyer, a young man from one of my witnessing teams, and we went out to a place called Grassy Park. There we found another little boy in almost the same condition as Collin Groves, and in the same kind of brace. From the hips down, he was wrapped with bandages which held him securely to the iron frame.

"He's got TB of the joints and spine," his mother told us. "He hasn't walked for eighteen months. Will you pray for him?"

"Yes," I said, "but where's his father?"

"At home," she said. "He's got no use for this kind of religion. He says he's a Christian, but all he does is sit at home and drink."

"Okay, we'll pray for the boy," I told her. Then Peter and I laid our hands on him and prayed, while that mother pleaded with God along with us.

As soon as I was through praying, that little

mother began unwrapping the bandages. While she was doing that, I went on ministering to other people who were waiting. In a few minutes, I heard a shout, and I turned to see that boy dancing a jig and praising God. As soon as the rest saw what had happened, they started praising God, too.

"I'm going home and show my father!" the boy said. So we all followed him to see what would happen. I'll never forget that scene. We had to walk over sand for about 300 yards, which is the worst kind of walking to do if you have any affliction of the legs or spine. But that boy walked along without a bit of hesitation. The neighbors heard us praising God, and stuck their heads out of their doors to see what was going on.

When we got to the boy's home, we went in and there was the father sitting there with a bottle of beer in his hand.

"Daddy!" the boy cried. "Look! I can walk! Jesus healed me!"

That father took one look at the boy and cried out, "Oh, my God! I don't believe it!"

I walked up to that father and put my arm around his shoulders. "Jesus loves you, buddy," I said. "Wouldn't you like to know Him?" He stood there and cried real tears of repentance.

A few days later, I was told that two male nurses from the big Victoria Hospital in Wynberg went out to tend to the boy, as they customarily did twice a week. When they saw him, they were very upset.

"We told you this boy must stay in that brace!" they said. "Why is he walking around like this?"

"A man of God prayed for him," the mother explained. "And through the power of God, he is walking, as you see."

"There's something wrong," they said. "You'll have to let us check him over."

So they got out their tape measures and carefully measured his hips and legs. Then they put him through a series of maneuvers to see if there was any pain in his joints. Finally, somewhat perplexed, they measured him again.

"Well," the mother said, "what about it? Must I put him back in the brace?"

"No," one of them said, "I guess he won't need that anymore."

"Wonderful! Praise the Lord!"

"Are you sure you haven't had any trouble with him since the brace was removed?" the other one asked.

"Trouble?" she asked. "Why, yes. Yesterday I had to beat him."

"Beat him? How did you beat him?"

"On the rump—how else?"

"But what for?"

"For climbing that big tree over there."

They looked at each other in amazement. They both knew that tree climbing would be physically impossible for a boy with such a painful disease.

"All right," they said, "the only advice we can give you is, if this doesn't last, you'd better sue the healer." They didn't quite understand that the Healer was the Lord Jesus.

CHAPTER THIRTEEN

SWEET OLD BOSWORTH

One day early in 1952, I said to Joyce, "I think it's time for my *rendezvous* with Bosworth."

"What *rendezvous?*" she asked, wrinkling her forehead in puzzlement.

"Don't you remember?" I replied. "I told you when I came back from Johannesburg last October that Bosworth had invited me to visit him in America."

"Oh, yes, you *did* mention that, didn't you?" she recalled. "I guess I wasn't paying much attention at the time."

"Well, I think God wants me to make that trip."

"But why? You've got enough to do here, haven't you?"

"Yes," I smiled, "but I just have a feeling that God's got some things to teach me through that old man, that's all."

Ever since Bosworth had made that suggestion four months previously, I hadn't been able to get the idea out of my mind. Even though God had been blessing my ministry in South Africa, still I felt I had much maturing to do. My years in the service had made me intensely overbearing and at times a little curt. I knew how badly I needed to be in the fellowship of an older, more mellow Christian brother, so I could learn more about the expression of the Christian graces in my own life and ministry.

So I sat down and wrote a letter to Bosworth at his home in Coral Gables, Florida, and mailed it off that afternoon. In a matter of days I received his reply. He said he'd soon be having a crusade in Hammond, Indiana, and that I should plan to meet him there.

A few weeks later, I landed at the big airport in Chicago and called the hotel where Bosworth was to be staying. As soon as he heard my voice and my South African accent, he knew who I was.

"Brother Thom!" he exclaimed. "Welcome to America!"

"Thank you," I replied. "I've been looking forward to coming."

"And how long are you planning to stay?" he inquired.

"A few weeks," I replied. "Is that all right?"

"Excellent!" he said. "I suggest you get a room in the same hotel where I'm staying, so we can fellowship as much as possible. We'll be busy in the meetings much of the time, but we simply *must* get together for some personal talks and times of prayer. Will you be coming right over?"

"Yes," I said. "I should be there within the hour."

"All right," he replied. "I'll be waiting for you."

That evening after I'd checked in, I felt a little nervous as I knocked on Bosworth's door. But the nervousness soon vanished when he answered the door and welcomed me so warmly. We sat down to talk, and it was as though we'd known one another for years. I'll never forget that evening. There was a spiritual "sweetness" about that old man that I had rarely seen in any Christian anywhere.

147

The next day we began the big crusade in Hammond, on the outskirts of Chicago. I helped by praying for the sick and leading people to Christ at invitation times. It was a real thrill to have a small part in those great meetings, and to have the opportunity of learning so much from this experienced "warrior of the cross."

After several more stops in the State of Indiana, we flew down to Miami, Florida, for another large crusade in a big Christian and Missionary Alliance Church where a Dr. Miller was the minister. They had a daily radio ministry which originated from the church auditorium; Dr. Miller decided to invite Bosworth or one of his associates to speak on the broadcasts. This, we all felt, would be excellent publicity for the crusade.

But imagine my surprise when Bosworth asked *me* if I'd take this responsibility!

"Who? Me?" I replied. "Why, I've never preached on the air before."

"No," Bosworth said, grinning, "but by tomorrow afternoon, that will no longer be true."

So the next morning, I went down to the church with Bosworth, who decided to sit up in the control room and watch while I worked on the platform with Dr. Miller.

When it came time for me to speak, I was shaking like a leaf in the wind. "Lord, You've got to help me," I prayed under my breath. "I don't know anything about this kind of preaching."

The fact that this was my first radio experience was bad enough; but as soon as I opened my mouth to speak, I realized I had to preach to an empty church—and that was worse!

But as I was struggling with my opening sentences, suddenly a peculiar vision came before me. I wanted to fight it off. I was trying to concentrate on my sermon. But it refused to go away. I saw a young soldier in the heat of the battle front in Korea. (Those were the days of the Korean war.) I heard the firing of artillery, and saw the boy was in danger. Then, quickly, the vision changed, and I saw the boy's mother putting a roast into the oven. I saw the worried expression on her face, and knew how burdened she must be for her son.

In a flash, I knew what God wanted me to say. "There's a mother listening to me right now who's putting a roast into the oven," I declared. "You've got a son on the battle front in Korea. You're carrying a burden of concern for that boy. You've wept many tears. But listen to me; I have a word from the Lord for you. Mother, let not your heart be troubled: you believe in God; believe also in Me. . . ."

For the next twenty-five minutes, I spoke to that mother as though face to face. I could see her in my vision, and God was telling me what to say to her.

When I finished, phone calls began to come in from all over Miami.

"Who was that preacher?" they inquired. "We never heard anything like *that!*" Even a newspaper reporter called.

Bosworth came down out of the control room with tears in his eyes. "Where did you ever learn to preach like that?" he asked.

"Well, I don't know," I replied. "I just saw a vision of a troubled mother, and I saw her boy in an American GI uniform, and I just knew I was supposed to talk to that mother."

149

"This is great!" Bosworth exclaimed. "I've never seen a finer demonstration of the word of knowledge."

Immediately, my mind went back to that day when I was baptized in the Spirit in McQuade's house. I remembered how I had seen the Lord in vision and how He had said to me, "*I give you the word of knowledge.*" Could it be that this promise was now beginning to be fulfilled? I had often read 1 Corinthians 12, and knew that one of the gifts of the Holy Spirit is "the word of knowledge." If I understood this gift correctly, it involved the "knowing" of certain facts by divine revelation. Hadn't Peter received a word of knowledge when God revealed to him the facts about Ananias's and Sapphira's deception? And if God had revealed that to Peter, then obviously He could give *me* knowledge about a worried mother. Why not? It seemed perfectly logical to me.

From that day on, Bosworth began to spend more and more time with me. He treated me as though I were his own son. Sometimes he took me to his home in Coral Gables and we would spend long evenings talking about the things of God. At other times, we would pray together, asking God's guidance for my ministry when I returned to Africa. A number of times he arranged speaking engagements for me, and always came to hear me preach. What a privilege it was to associate with this great man!

One evening he brought up a subject that surprised me somewhat. "Robert," he said, "I believe God's hand is upon you. He's given you a great ministry. But you need to be ordained."

"Ordained?" I replied. "You're joking, aren't

you? I have no formal training for the ministry—what good is ordination going to do?"

"A great deal of good, Robert," he insisted. "There are some doors that will remain forever closed to you if you're not a duly recognized minister of the Gospel. There are many pulpits where you'll not be welcomed and many people who'll not respect your ministry."

"Are you suggesting that I go back to school then?" I asked a little apprehensively.

"Not really," he replied with a smile. "If you were a younger man, I'd say yes. But you're thirty-seven, and God's already launched you into a good ministry."

"But you still think I should be ordained?"

"Yes," he replied. "I think that's very important."

"But I can still be a minister *without* ordination, can't I?"

"In a way. It's like a pitcher having big league pitching abilities and yet not being recognized by the big leagues. And a pitcher like that can pitch pro ball in all the minor leagues he wants to, but he'll never really make the grade as a big league pitcher until some scout recognizes him and helps get him hired."

"So what scout will recognize me?" I chuckled.

"This scout right here."

"You?"

"Yes, Brother. I've watched your ministry and I believe you've got the necessary qualifications. I'm about ready to recommend you to a 'club.'"

"But what General Manager would hire *me?*"

"Ah," he said with a warm smile, "I know just the man. We'll write to my good friend, Joseph

Mattsson-Boze up in Chicago. He's the pastor of the Independent Assembly of God there. He'll be glad to arrange for your ordination, I'm sure."

So within a couple of weeks, we flew up to Mattsson-Boze's church where a special ordination ceremony was held for me. Henry Carlson, one of the international directors of the Full Gospel Businessmen's Fellowship was there, and a Mrs. Mary Uzelle, who had an unusual prophetic ministry in that church. When the time came for them to lay their hands on me, Brother Carlson began to pray in tongues. Mrs. Uzelle gave the interpretation, and I felt the powerful anointing of God coming upon me as she spoke these words:

> *Thus saith the Lord, My eyes searched the nation and looked among the people to find a man that would go and stand in the breach. Have I not lifted thee from the lowest level that a man could fall? Have I not delivered thee? Have I not set thee free? Yea, behold, I have given unto thee the gift of faith, and great shall it be. . . .*

> *Behold I am the Lord thy God, and I have given thee the gift to drive out demons. Thou shalt also lay hands on the sick, and they shall recover. And I, the Lord, shall provide for all thy needs, and great shall be thy faith.*

When the interpretation was finished, I was in tears. Brother Mattsson-Boze came and put his arm around my shoulder. "Bless you, Robert," he said. "This is just the beginning."

152

The next day, I was eating lunch with Bosworth when he said to me, "Robert, I'd like to go to Africa with you."

"With me?" I said in surprise. "What do you mean?"

"We could work together for a while. I'm scheduled to begin a few campaigns in South Africa next month. Why don't you go along and be my Man Friday? Maybe this will help get you launched into an even greater ministry."

"It sounds very enticing," I replied, "but let me pray a few days before I make up my mind."

A few weeks later, I was on a ship with the seventy-five-year-old Bosworth, heading back to Cape Town. After a few exciting days with Joyce and the kids, we went by car to Carnarvon to begin our first campaign. For the duration of that revival, and for the next ten months, I was Bosworth's constant companion. I shared a room with him wherever we went. Every night he'd ask me to place six sharpened pencils and a long writing tablet beside his bed.

"What're they for?" I asked quizzically on the first night.

"The Lord gives me my sermons at night," he explained, "and I just write down what He gives me."

I had never heard of this method of sermon preparation before, so I was hoping I'd get to see him in action. Sure enough, about a half hour after he'd gone to sleep, the Holy Spirit woke him up and he sat up and began writing like mad. After a few minutes, he turned the light out and went back to sleep. But not for long. In another twenty minutes or so, the light was back on and I heard him writing away. Before morning, he must have been awakened ten or twelve times.

At seven o'clock the next morning, he was up. He came over to my bed with his long tablet in hand. "Look here, Robert," he said. "Here's the sermon the Holy Ghost gave me during the night."

I took the tablet, and there it was: a perfect sermon, completely organized and fully fortified with many Scripture passages.

"What a way to get a sermon!" I said. "Aren't you tired?"

"Tired?" he chuckled. "Whoever got tired listening to the Holy Ghost?"

For ten months I watched that old man get his sermons that way. And when the time came for him to preach, God's anointing would come upon him in such power that great congregations sat spellbound under his preaching and thousands came to know Jesus through his ministry.

My all-too-brief association with Bosworth did indeed launch me into a new phase of ministry. I soon began traveling to more and more distant places to preach the Gospel, and was often away from home for months at a time.

I can't say this was easy. But throughout the months spent with Bosworth, I'd learned a great deal about the depth of consecration required to take up one's cross and follow Jesus. Every night I'd hear that old man calling out his wife's name in prayer, and I knew how much he missed her, just as I missed being with Joyce. Yet I saw how willingly he made this sacrifice for the sake of Jesus. So I soon learned that God wanted me to be at His disposal, willing to be sent wherever He wanted me to go.

Joyce was a real princess through all those early years of my ministry. I knew my many trips were hard on her, but there was never a word of complaint. Always, she would be at home praying for me, trying to be both a mother and a father to the children. We discussed and prayed over every trip I made, and when it became clear to both of us that I was to be off again, she always agreed.

Few people understand the special problems that face a couple living this kind of life. It was difficult for me to maintain the kind of family togetherness that I wanted, but God showed me a few things I could do. Though it was costly, I began to make it a practice to keep in touch with Joyce by telephone as often as possible. We'd lived by faith ever since I'd been in the ministry, so I was confident that God would supply this need for the sake of our family. And how I looked forward to those conversations with Joyce! But I was always a little amused when she asked me the same question every month: "Honey, how are we going to pay the rent *this month?*"

I also decided that once every two years I would take my whole family with me on a three or four month missionary tour. This did much to strengthen our family ties and give the children a better understanding of what I was doing. Through the years, we made many trips together, all over America and Europe.

But there were times of severe testing. The ministry among the people of the Cape wasn't so bad; that was home. But the many trips abroad were often distressing.

I'll never forget the time I had to make a quick flight home. Joyce had phoned me that Lionel, our second oldest boy, had had a serious accident and was in the hospital.

When I arrived at the Groot Schuur Hospital, there was Joyce almost in hysteria. Lionel had been playing with firecrackers. Twenty-five of them had exploded in his back pocket. There were extensive internal injuries. The doctors said that only an emergency operation could save his life.

Immediately the devil whispered to me, "If you had been home being a father to that boy, this wouldn't have happened." I took Joyce's hand and we prayed definitely that God would touch Lionel.

He was injured so badly that he couldn't be moved from his bed to the operating table. So they set up an emergency operating theater around his bed, while one of the doctors presented me with a paper to sign.

"This form gives us permission to perform surgery," the doctor explained. "Since he's under age, we'll need your signature."

"Doctor," I said, "I'll not sign that paper until I've first laid my hands on my son and prayed for him."

"There's no time for that!" the doctor warned. "Don't you realize this boy's dying?"

"I know that," I said. "Let me lay my hands on him."

"Sign the paper!" the doctor demanded.

"I cannot until I've prayed."

At that, the doctor stalked away angrily and was soon back with one of the chief medics of the hospital.

"Mr. Thom," the medic said, "if you don't sign that paper, and the boy dies, I'll have you arrested!"

"But I've asked this doctor to let me lay my hands on my son and pray before the operation," I insisted. "Surely you can grant me that small favor."

He looked at me with disdain. "I'll give you two minutes to pray for him," he snapped.

When I approached Lionel's bed, I saw what agony he was in. "Son," I said, "I'm going to do what I believe; I'm going to lay my hands on you in the name of the Lord Jesus Christ—and then I'm going back to sign that paper as the law demands." Then I simply laid my hands on his trembling body and prayed a simple prayer of faith, claiming his healing according to the Word of God. As I walked away from his bed, I "heard" God say to me, *"I am the Lord thy God who healeth all thy diseases."*

As soon as I left the room, the doctors and nurses hurried in to begin their work. I watched for a moment as they went in. As soon as the door was shut, I bowed my head there in that corridor and began to praise God. I knew God had heard my prayer.

"How is he?" Joyce wanted to know, when I got back to the waiting room.

"He'll be all right," I said confidently.

Just then, Joyce looked over my shoulder and gasped. I turned to see a group of doctors coming toward us. They were the very same doctors I had seen hurrying into Lionel's room just minutes before. Quickly, I went to meet them.

"What's wrong?" I asked.

The devil whispered, "He's dead!"

"Well, Mr. Thom," the chief medic said with an ashen face, "I don't know exactly how to explain this, but when we lifted the bed cover from your son, there was no sign of the wound, except for a small scar. . . ."

I couldn't help grinning broadly. "I can explain that, Doctor. You're too slow! Doctor Jesus finished the job while you were waiting in the corridor!"

Later on, I said to Joyce, "I just wish sweet old Bosworth could have been here to see the expression on those doctors' faces!"

"Yes," Joyce replied, "he'd have died laughing!"

CHAPTER FOURTEEN

ONE GENERATOR WITH MUSTARD AND MAYONNAISE

In 1956, I made another trip to America, but this time alone. I had received invitations to speak at many churches, and in a number of Full Gospel Businessmen's conventions.

While I was at the convention in Minneapolis, I began to feel a great burden for our work among the poor people of the Cape back in Africa. We had been adding more and more witnessing teams to our group, and distributing thousands of books. But still there were multitudes who were unreached with the Gospel. It came to me while I was praying that I could do a better job of evangelizing if I had another electric generator. I knew from previous experience what crowds would come to a lit-up field where the Gospel was being preached.

As I prayed, I saw a vision. It was like a "picture" passing before my eyes—a picture of a portable Holman generator. It was green, 110-115 volts, 1500 watts, and was priced at $300.

My first inclination was to get on the telephone immediately and try to locate such a generator. But as I picked up the phone book and began to turn to the yellow pages, God seemed to say, *"No, you are not required to search for this generator. Trust Me, and I will lead you to it."* So I put the phone book down and left the matter in God's hands. However, on a hunch that I would soon be needing the information I had seen in the vision, I jotted the details down in a little notebook, and put it in my inside coat pocket.

In a few days, I left Minneapolis and flew down to Fort Worth, Texas, to speak in another convention. After one of the services, a group of Christian men were sitting around a table in a restaurant talking to me about our work in Africa.

"We'd sure like to help you," one of the men spoke up. "Is there anything you need?"

"Well, yes," I admitted. "I need an electric generator."

"You know what kind?"

"Yes. I need a Holman, 110-115 volts, 1500 watts. God showed me that in a vision."

"He did? When?"

"Just a few days ago. I know exactly what it looks like, and I even know how much it'll cost me."

"Say!" one of the men cut in. "There's a fellow downtown who runs an army surplus store. Why don't we go down and see him? Maybe he's got a good generator for sale."

They all agreed that we ought to go immediately, and since it wasn't my idea, I consented to go along just in case this might be God's leading.

When we arrived at the store, one of my friends told the owner we were looking for a portable power plant.

"Yes, sir!" he said. "What size do you need?"

"Just a small one," I replied, not wanting to divulge the details at that point. "Why don't you show us what you have?"

"Okay," the owner agreed. "I think I've got exactly what you need right back here." And he took us into another room and showed us a rather large generator painted bright red.

"Ain't she a beauty?" he said, smiling.

"Yes, it's a nice one, all right," I replied, "but I can't take it."

"But wait'll you hear the price!" he said, still smiling. "You can have this generator for $375—and that's the best portable I've got."

"No," I said, "it isn't the right color."

I guess he thought I was joking because he completely ignored what I said and offered me a lower price.

"Three-fifty?"

"No, I can't take it."

"Three-forty-five?"

"No, you don't understand. It's not the right color. Is this all you have?"

"Oh, no," he said. "I got more. Look over here—how's this one?"

It was painted gray.

"No," I said, "that's not the right color either. Don't you have another one?"

He looked at me as though I were some kind of crackpot. "Well, I got this orange one here, and here's another red one—and this blue one. Do you like any of those colors?"

"No," I said, "none of these will do. There's one more you haven't shown me."

"No," he said, "you've seen all my portables."

"Are you sure?"

Just then, one of the fellows who'd come with me yelled out, "Hey, you guys, here's one stuck away back here!"

"Oh, yeah," the store owner said, "I forgot all about *that* one!" He went back to pull it out where we could all see it. Immediately, I reached into my coat pocket and pulled out my little notebook.

"Watch this, now," I said to the men, and I held up the open notebook in front of my face.

"All right, sir," I said. "I've got my little notebook here, and I've got written down what I need. What type of plant is that?"

"Holman."

"Okay, what's the color?"

"Green."

"What's the voltage?"

"110-115 volts."

"What's the wattage?"

"1.5 kilowatts."

"What's that in watts?"

"Fifteen hundred watts."

"Okay, what's the price?"

"You tell *me*."

"No, you tell *me*."

"Okay, $300."

With a broad smile on my face, I walked over to that man and handed him my little notebook. "Friend," I said, "will you kindly read what's in my book? This is what God told me just a few days ago." He glanced down over my list of specifications and shook his head in amazement.

I had that power plant shipped back to Africa, knowing how valuable it would be in the many open-air meetings I would be having when I returned to Capetown.

However, there was still one big problem facing me. How was I going to transport that generator from place to place, once it arrived in Africa? I had no automobile. Cars were very hard to come by in Africa. As long as I had been in the service, I had been permitted to use Army vehicles. But now that I was on my own, I had to walk or hitchhike everywhere I went.

The more I thought about it, the more I realized what a worthless piece of equipment that generator would be without a car. So I decided that I'd apply to the government for a special import permit when I got back to Africa, so I could buy an American-made car.

Many of my friends told me how hard it was to get these permits. Only the most important people were permitted to import cars, I was told, and unless I had some government official to pull some strings for me, it would be completely out of the question.

One of my friends gave me the name of a Christian senator who would be able to help me. But as I prayed about how to proceed, God seemed to say to me, *"All you need to do is ask Me; you don't need to connive; if you just ask in My name, I will do it."*

So I decided against talking to the senator, and instead went directly to the government import office and asked for an application for an import permit. On that application, I wrote that I wanted one Chevrolet motor car, 1956 model, colors gold and yellow. Then I went home and told Joyce what I had done.

"Gold and yellow?" she cackled. "Why such crazy colors?"

"What's the matter," I teased. "Don't you like mustard and mayonnaise?"

"Bob," she laughed, "whoever heard of a preacher

driving something like that? Why, I'll bet they don't even *make* a car that color."

"Oh, yes they do," I replied. "I saw one on my last trip to the States, and I made up my mind right then and there that that's the kind of car I wanted!"

She flopped down in the big living room chair and laughed until the tears came. "Oh, Bob," she said between laughs, "you're just too much!"

Well, it didn't seem very likely that I'd get the permit anyway, but I had the promise of God so I kept holding on in faith. While I was waiting, I happened to meet a missionary one day who was trying to get a permit to import a truck.

"You know," he said, "these permits are worth their weight in gold these days."

"Yes, I know," I replied. "Do you expect to get yours?"

"Well, it'll be difficult," he replied, "but I've got a Christian senator working for me, so maybe it's not hopeless."

When I questioned him further, I found out that the senator was the same one who'd been recommended to me by my friend.

"Well," I said, "I've got an application in too, but I put mine straight through the import office."

"You did?" the missionary chuckled. "You know where that application will end up?"

"No, where?"

"In the wastebasket!"

It sounded discouraging, but I kept praising God for that permit. About two weeks after I submitted the application, I received a letter from the import office. When I opened the envelope, there was the permit.

"Here it is!" I shouted to Joyce.

"Is that really the permit?" she asked in disbelief.

"Yep. God's going to give us a car!"

"Uh-oh," she said. "Here comes the mustard and mayonnaise!"

"You'd better believe it," I chuckled. "God gives me what I ask for!"

Now that I had the permit, I was ready to face the next big hurdle. And a *big* hurdle it was! I had a permit, but no money.

"How can you ever *think* of getting a car without money?" the devil mocked. Not having any sensible answer to that question, I decided to ignore the thought and leave it up to God to work out the details.

Later on in that year of 1956, I made another trip to the States. This time I met a good Christian friend, Albert Seitz, who offered to drive me wherever I wanted to go in his truck. So for two and a half months, I rode all over the country in that truck. Every time we passed a gold and yellow Chevrolet, I'd say right out loud, "Thank You, Lord, that's the color car I want."

Albert would laugh and say, "Do you really believe you're going to get it?"

"Sure I do," I replied. "God told me!"

Finally we arrived in Hampton, Iowa, and Albert had to return home. He dropped me off at the home of a Christian brother by the name of Floyd Methfessel, who was to drive me on to Minneapolis, where I was to preach at a Full Gospel Businessmen's convention the next day.

Within an hour, Floyd was ready to start the trip. As soon as we were on the highway, he wanted to know all about the work I was doing for the Lord in Africa. I explained to him all about our witnessing teams and open-air meetings. and how we often hitchhiked from place to place.

"Brother Thom," he said, "you need a car in Africa, don't you?"

"Oh, yes," I said, "but the Lord's going to provide. I've already asked him for a new Chevrolet."

"Oh, is that right?" he said. "And what color would you like your new Chevrolet to be?"

"Gold and yellow," I said. "Mustard and mayonnaise."

He laughed right out loud. "Over here most preachers drive *black* cars," he said.

"I know," I said, "but I like gold and yellow better."

"Well, everybody to their own taste," he chuckled.

When we arrived at my hotel in Minneapolis, Floyd said to me, "Brother Thom, I want you to come back to visit me in a couple of months. Would that be possible?"

"Well, I think so," I replied, pulling my date book out of my pocket. "Let's see—yes, I can be back at your place ten weeks from today."

"Good!" he exclaimed. "I'll be looking forward to your visit!" And with that we parted.

The next day the Full Gospel Businessmen's convention began in the very hotel where I was staying. There were a number of outstanding speakers who ministered during the week, and the Holy Spirit was poured out upon many people. I'll never forget one meeting in particular. Demos Shakarian, president of the Full Gospel Businessmen's Fellowship International, was there that night. Also present was Dr. Mordecai Ham, the

Baptist evangelist who had led Billy Graham to Christ.

At the close of the service, the regular invitation was given for any inquirers to go to a room which had been designated as a prayer room. As soon as the invitation was given, I quickly made my way to the prayer room to help in whatever way I could. But to my surprise, the room was so full I could only stand in the doorway and pray quietly for those within. After I'd prayed for a while, I lifted my head and was a little surprised to find Mordecai Ham standing there beside me, watching all that was going on!

Many, many people in that prayer room received the baptism in the Spirit that night and spoke in tongues. Among them were quite a number of Lutheran ministers—and in 1956 that was practically unheard-of. As the Holy Spirit fell on these people, Mordecai Ham turned to me, weeping. "To think," he said, "that I've fought the manifestation of tongues for nearly sixty years!"

I went back to my room that evening rejoicing in Spirit. "Lord," I said within myself, "this is marvelous! All kinds of people are opening up to the Holy Spirit!"

From that convention, I went on to many other meetings and witnessed hundreds of miracles of salvation and healing. But finally the ten weeks rolled by, and I knew I must be going back to Floyd Methfessel's home in Iowa, as previously promised.

Actually, I had no idea why I should make this return trip to Floyd's home, but God seemed to assure me that it was His will. And that assurance was underscored when I again crossed paths with Albert

Seitz and his truck, and he offered to take me to Floyd's home once more!

It was around midnight when we pulled into Floyd's driveway, and the house was dark. As Albert hopped out of the truck, he said, "You stay here—I'll see if I can get them up." He left the truck running and disappeared into the darkness.

Feeling quite tired from the long drive, I decided to get out for a stretch. The headlights of the truck were shining on the doors of Floyd's big double garage. Idly, I peered through the glass panels of those garage doors. There, by the illumination of the headlights, I saw a gold and yellow Chevrolet. . . .

In a few minutes, Albert was back out unloading my luggage and getting it into the house. As soon as that was done and we were inside the house and had exchanged greetings, Floyd said to me, "You looked into the garage, didn't you?"

"Yes," I admitted, grinning.

"And what did you see?"

"I saw a Chevrolet there—a gold and yellow Chevrolet."

"That's right," he said. "That's *your* car! The Lord told me to get it for you!"

My eyes filled up with tears of joy as he led me downstairs to the garage and handed me the keys. "There it is," he said. "Get in. It's all yours."

When I got behind the steering wheel of that brand new car, all I could do was bow my head and say tearfully, "Thank You, Jesus! Thank You! Thank You!"

When I returned to Africa, I immediately put my "mustard and mayonnaise" car to use. I hitched up my generator and drove out to many villages to preach the Gospel in open fields. Multitudes of people came, as much to see the car and the electric lights as to hear the Gospel. But God honored His Word and thousands were saved and healed.

One night, we held a meeting in Athlone, a suburb of Cape Town. Unknown to me, there was a Mrs. Beades in the meeting, a backslidden Christian who had a torn bladder. Six years before, a gangster had broken into her second floor apartment; she ran into the bathroom and slammed the door shut. Frantically, she tried to crawl out of the window, but fell and injured herself severely. She was rushed to the hospital where she was X-rayed promptly. The pictures showed a torn bladder and several fractured bones. But not having sufficient money to have surgery at that time, she asked to be sent home to recover as best she could.

The sad result of that accident was that she could retain very little liquid from that time on. For six years she had not dared drink a cup of coffee or tea before going to bed. Nor had she been able to go to church—or anywhere else, for that matter. It was a miracle that she had survived; but apparently God was sparing her and giving her time to get out of her backslidden state.

Then came that night when Mrs. Beades came to our meeting in Athlone. As she sat there listening, I said, "If there's anyone here who wants to get right with the Lord tonight, rise to your feet; I'm going to pray for you." She stood to her feet, along with many others, and came back to the Lord.

After the prayer I said, "Now if there's anyone here who's sick, step up front; I'll be praying for the sick in a few minutes."

But she just stood there, rooted to the spot. It was hard for her to believe in "this healing business." Her church had taught her that the days of miracles are past, and that healing is not for today. So she decided she'd just stand there and watch.

The next night she was back. When I gave the invitation for healing, she was among the first to come forward. When it came her turn to be prayed for, I said, "Madam, what is it you want to be healed of?"

"Sir," she replied, "I haven't come to be prayed for; I've come to tell you and all these people here that *last night* I had a wonderful healing."

"Last night?" I couldn't remember praying for her.

"Yes," she said. "I just want to tell you that last night I came in here with a torn bladder. I had been able to retain only a very little liquid in my body for six years. But last night while you were praying for the others, something strange happened. I felt an unseen hand massaging my bladder. . . ." At that she began to cry.

I had never heard anything quite like this before. "Tell us exactly how it felt," I said, probing for more information.

"Oh," she said, smiling through her tears, "it was actually embarrassing! It just felt like warm fingers gently massaging my bladder. I can't explain it any better than that. All I know is that I went home and had a cup of coffee with my husband before going to bed—which is something I haven't done in six years."

"And it didn't bother you?"

"No. I never got up all night. So when I woke up this morning, I realized I had been healed."

"And you had a torn bladder?"

"Yes," she said, "my file is over at Groot Schuur Hospital. I'm supposed to be X-rayed again on Tuesday for possible surgery."

As I stood there talking with her, God showed me that though her bladder was healed, she was still suffering from the fractures, which hadn't healed properly. So I simply laid my hands on her and pronounced her fully healed in the name of Jesus. She trembled under the power of God.

"Now," I said, "what happened?"

"Oh!" she exclaimed. "I felt that hand again massaging my bones! I heard them click back into place!"

On Tuesday, Mrs. Beades later told me, she went up to the hospital for her X-rays. While she was in the waiting room, she began to tell the other outpatients about what had happened. After a while, a couple of doctors overheard the conversation and they said to her, "Madam, you're upsetting the other patients. Come with us."

So they took her into a room and offered her a chair. "Now, then," they said, "tell *us* the story you were telling those people out there."

So she repeated the whole thing as they listened skeptically. Finally the older of the two said to the younger, "Get her file."

When the files were brought, they found the X-rays that showed the fractures and the torn bladder. "But we won't know if there's been any change until we've taken new X-rays," the older doctor said.

So she went to the X-ray room, and then waited in a consultation room for the report. After about an hour, the doctor walked in and looked at Mrs.

Beades silently for a moment. Finally he spoke up very abruptly: "You can go home, Mrs. Beades; you've been healed."

"Praise the Lord!" she laughed. "What did I tell you?"

The doctor grinned sheepishly as she left the room.

When Mrs. Beades told me this story several days later, I said under my breath, "Thank you, Lord, for a generator and one mustard and mayonnaise car!"

CHAPTER FIFTEEN

SAFARI TO TONETTI

•
_____

By 1959, I had purchased a big green tent, 60′ x 120′, which proved to be an ideal place to have our meetings. After we pitched the tent in many places in and around Cape Town, it seemed that God was telling me to take my family on an extended tour of South Africa. My goal was to reach a place called Tonetti, about 1200 miles away, far up in the northeast corner of South Africa. It was an area of great spiritual darkness, where the people listened to the advice of witch doctors and worshipped demons.

When I casually suggested to Joyce that she and the children come along, their faces lit up with delight.

"What a good idea!" Joyce exclaimed. "How far will we be going?"

"Twelve or thirteen hundred miles. A place called Tonetti, up around Kruger National Park."

"But that's lion country, isn't it?" She looked suddenly worried.

"Yes. Snake country, too."

"I could think of better places to go camping."

"But none quite so exciting, my dear," I teased.

The kids were all chattering at once. Lions and snakes sounded exciting to them. But Joyce wasn't quite so sure.

"It'll be all right," I assured her. "We won't be going through the park, so it'll be perfectly safe."

"All right," she said, resignedly. "If God wants us to go there. . . ."

So on the following week, Joyce and I and our six youngest children (we had eight by that time) jammed into our yellow and gold Chevrolet and headed north, pulling our tent and generator behind us.

It was a long, tiresome journey which took several days. At night, we'd stop along the way and pitch a small tent we'd brought along for camping. At daybreak, we'd all be up for breakfast over an open fire, before starting off again.

When we finally pulled into the native village of Tonetti on the fourth day, black people came running from everywhere to see the "golden wonder." They especially liked the chrome, and fingered it with delight, chattering among themselves in a language I didn't understand.

I had been told that there was a woman missionary working in Tonetti—a Miss Stacey, who was serving under the British Assemblies of God Mission Board. Both Joyce and I were eager to meet Miss Stacey and see what we could do to help. We had some difficulty making the natives understand what we wanted, but when we said the name "Stacey" three or four times, their faces lit up and they motioned for us to follow them.

Miss Stacey was a small but energetic woman who had great compassion for the needs of the people in Tonetti. As soon as she found out who we were, why we had come, and that we had a tent and electric generator, she was overjoyed.

"This is an answer to my prayers," she said with beaming face. "The work here has been slow—just

174

a convert now and then. But what we need is a way of reaching many of them at once."

"Well," I said, "let's set up the tent and see what happens. I predict we'll be packed out at every service."

"I *believe* it!" she sang out. "God's going to give us a *revival!*"

"By the way," I said, "can you supply us with an interpreter?"

"Yes," she replied, "we have a young man. Danielli is his name. I'll ask him to help."

We prayed together for a few minutes, thanking God for bringing us together and for the revival He was going to send. Then we set out to find a clearing large enough to set up the big tent.

It didn't take us long. Even the kids pitched in to help, and by late afternoon we had the tent set up and wired for lights. Large crowds of natives stood around curiously, watching us work. I asked Miss Stacey to tell them about the services we were going to have.

That night, there was an overflow crowd in and around the tent long before the service was to begin. When I started up the generator and the lights came on, they squealed with delight.

When the time came for me to preach, Danielli was there at my side. As soon as we began, I knew Miss Stacey had made a wise choice. Every statement I made was interpreted with great power and anointing. At times, tears rolled down his cheeks as he spoke. When we gave the invitation, many of the natives responded, accepting Jesus as their Savior.

We also prayed for the sick during those meetings. Danielli prayed along with me, and oh, the love and compassion that flowed out of his heart!

After the service, I said to Miss Stacey, "That young man, Danielli—I've never seen anything like him. Was he born in a missionary home, or where did he get all that power?"

"No, Brother Thom," Miss Stacey answered, "Danielli was born right out here in the bush country. His brother is a missionary about six miles from here, but Danielli had very bad beginnings."

"Oh? What do you mean?"

"He studied for five years to be a witch doctor."

"A witch doctor? That's unbelievable! How did he become a Christian?"

"Well, that's an interesting story. On the night of his graduation from witch doctor's training, which was held on a Saturday night at midnight, the instructors told Danielli that *Satani* would come into him twenty-four hours later."

"Who's Satani?" I interrupted.

"That's the native name for Satan. They told him Satani would come as a flame of fire and take possession of him. He was to stand outside his hut at midnight, and when he saw the fire coming, he was to open his mouth, and Satani would enter him."

"And that would give him supernatural powers, I suppose?"

"Yes, they told him that he would receive the power of life and death."

"So what happened?"

"Well, the next night, he did as he was told. Shortly before midnight he went out and stood in the darkness beside the door of his hut, waiting for the fire to appear. As he stood there, he began to be afraid. He thought about his missionary brother who had warned him repeatedly about the power of Satani. The longer he stood there, the more fearful he became."

"I'll bet his brother was praying for him," I commented.

"He was; he told us later. Well, anyway, as the hour of midnight came very close, suddenly Danielli said to himself, 'Here comes the fire!' It frightened him so, that his only thought was to get to his brother as fast as his legs would carry him. As he ran, he said he thought he could hear the devil right behind him."

"I wouldn't be surprised if it really was," I said. "The power of these witch doctors is more real than many people think."

"I know. I've seen it too. Well, Danielli ran for six miles up hill and down dale through that lion-and-snake-infested country, and when he got to his brother's hut, he almost collapsed as he cried out, 'Help me!' And his brother ran out, and he told us later that he felt the power of Satani all around. So he shouted, 'Satani, I rebuke you in the name of Jesus Christ! I command you to leave my brother alone! Go and come back no more!' "

"And then what happened?"

"Danielli said that instantly he felt that evil power leave, and he began to weep for joy. And in a few moments, his brother led him to Christ, and he also received the baptism in the Holy Ghost."

"Praise the Lord!" I whooped, clapping my hands together. "Isn't that wonderful!"

"Yes," Miss Stacey replied. "God's been good to Danielli. He'll be a great blessing in this revival."

Later that night, Joyce and I and the six kids all settled down for a night's rest in our little tent, 14' x 10′ x 6′. We slept in that tent every night. The kids thought it was great fun being packed in there like sardines. But there was a lot of tossing and turning, and you'd wake up in the morning wondering whose foot was almost in your mouth.

But it was lots of fun. Actually, we lived like kings. We could buy a big piece of meat for fifteen cents, and we'd get vegetables from farmers who lived around the area. We cooked over an open fire, and the natives were kind to us and brought many gifts of food. So we felt very blest, in spite of the minor discomforts of camping.

Night after night God's blessings were poured out on the services. Danielli was always at my side as we ministered to the people, and many, many people experienced the miracle of salvation. The great number of conversions was brought about, not only through the preaching of the Word, but also by the signs and miracles, which deeply impressed the people with the power of Jesus.

One night a woman came into the tent who was bent over so badly that her forehead almost touched the ground. She hobbled along with the aid of an old crooked stick, her head tilted upwards slightly. Her sunken eyes and shriveled but determined mouth were tell-tale signs of the difficult life she'd lived. Sure enough, when it came time to pray for the sick, this poor woman was in the healing line.

"Danielli," I said, "ask her how long she's been this way." There was a brief exchange between them.

"Nine years," he replied.

Immediately, Danielli and I laid our hands on her in the name of Jesus, and I said, "Ought not this

178

woman, bound these nine years by Satan, be loosed in Jesus' name?"

I said this remembering how Jesus, when confronted with a similar case, had said, "*Ought not this woman . . . whom Satan hath bound, lo, these eighteen years, be loosed from this bond . . . ?*" (Luke 13:16). But then it came to me that *that* woman's affliction had been caused by a *"spirit"* of infirmity, according to an earlier verse in the chapter.

Taking that as a clue to the cause of the condition of *this* woman, who was now before us, I said, "In the name of Jesus Christ, thou foul spirit of affliction, I command you to come out of her, and set her free right now!"

Immediately, she threw her stick to the ground, straightened up and began to dance for joy, perfectly whole in Jesus' name! Most of the people wept, and before that service was over, many natives received Jesus as their Savior.

"Oh, Brother Thom!" Miss Stacey exclaimed tearfully. "The revival I prayed for has come!"

During the revival the Lord delivered many people who were possessed of the devil. Some of these tormented people tried to break up the services, acting like animals and making strange noises. But when we rebuked these evil spirits in the name of Jesus, these people were perfectly delivered.

All too soon, though, the time came when I knew we must start the long journey home. Joyce was quite tired, and I knew the children were getting weary, too. So with mixed emotions, we took the tent down and bade everyone goodbye.

"I'll never forget these wonderful days," Miss

Stacey said with trembling lips. "This has truly been the work of the Holy Spirit!"

"Yes, and this is just the beginning," I replied. "As long as you've got young men like Danielli here, the work will go on." I then embraced Danielli as though he were my own son, got in the car and drove away, while thousands of natives waved farewell to us.

CHAPTER SIXTEEN

"GET THIS MAN OUT OF TOWN!"

We had planned to drive out to the east coast on our way home from Tonetti. This section of Africa was populated with many Hindus, and I felt it would be a real challenge to work among people who were known to be very resistant to Christian missionary efforts. Having previously communicated with a pastor in Melville by the name of Bobby Mannikim, who was himself a converted Hindu, we were eager to accept his invitation to preach the Gospel in that difficult community.

Melville was a busy sugar-manufacturing town. Most of the farmers around the outlying areas raised sugar cane, and sold it to the large factory for processing. As soon as we drove into this town, we knew we were in Hindu territory. Almost all of the women wore the Indian *sari*, and many animals roamed in the streets. Groups of men gazed with interest at our gold and yellow automobile as we went by.

It was a time of great rejoicing when we found Bobby Mannikim. Though we had never met before, we sensed a bond of Christian fellowship the moment we laid eyes on one another.

"Welcome to Melville, Brother Thom!" he sang out. "What a joy to have you here!"

I thanked him for the warm welcome, and introduced all the rest of my family. Then we stood around and chatted gaily about the revival we felt sure God was going to send. After the outpouring of God's Spirit at Tonetti, our faith was high for Melville.

The next day, Bobby helped us find a vacant lot where we could erect our tent. By mid-morning, we were hard at work setting the poles and unrolling the canvas. As we worked, I noticed many Hindus standing around, trying to figure out what we were doing.

By that evening, the word had gotten around all over town that we were having a revival. Many of the local Christians showed up for the first service; but to our disappointment, only a handful of Hindus came. Within a few days, however, miracles of healing began to take place, and more and more Hindus flocked into the tent to see what was going on.

When a few of the Hindus were actually converted, I knew we were in for trouble. We were being watched carefully by the Hindu priests, and they obviously felt threatened by our presence.

The crowds grew larger and larger. One morning, after we'd had an especially good service the night before, Bobby received a telephone call from one of the priests.

"Get this man out of town," the Hindu priest warned. "Otherwise we are going to kill him *tonight*." And without waiting for a reply, he hung up.

The color drained from Bobby's face. I knew something was wrong. "What's the matter?" I asked.

"They're threatening to kill you."

"Who?"

"The Hindu priests."

"But why?"

"You're making too many converts. They're very angry. Either you leave town immediately, or they're going to kill you."

"Tonight?"

"That's what the priest said. He was furious."

"What do you think I ought to do?"

"Maybe we'd better take the tent down and get you packed up. After all, you've got a family to think of."

I sat silently for a few moments, just thinking. "Bobby," I said finally, "give me an hour to pray. I feel like I need some guidance."

Finding a place where I could be alone, I laid the matter before God. "Lord, You sent me here on this mission, and now You see how I'm being threatened. What do You want me to do?"

As I prayed, God brought two passages of scripture to me very forcefully. *"Haven't I told you in My Word that the time would come that 'whosoever killeth you will think that he doeth God service'? And haven't I told you, 'rejoice, and be exceeding glad: for great is your reward in heaven: for so persecuted they the prophets which were before you'?"*

An hour later, I came back to Bobby with a big grin. "It's all right, Bobby," I said. "God sent me here to have a revival, and if it costs my life, we'll *have* one!"

That night, we went down to the tent as usual; there was an overflow crowd. As the time neared for me to speak, I sensed a powerful anointing of the Holy Spirit coming upon me. Surveying the crowd, I noticed a Hindu priest glaring at me from the back entrance of the tent. I assumed that this was the priest who'd called Bobby that morning. Then I noticed an especially large, muscular, Hindu man standing in the doorway to my left. I noticed that he and the priest kept exchanging glances.

"Well," I thought, "if that's the man they've picked to do the job, they've made a good choice."

I stood up to preach, not knowing whether I'd be gunned down, or whether that big man would plunge a knife into me after the service. I only knew he was there for no good.

"Lord," I prayed silently, "I commit myself to You. You take care of me and glorify Your Son Jesus."

That night I saw how willing the Lord is to honor faith and confirm His Word. The preaching was unusually plain and powerful, and when I gave the invitation, a number of Hindus came forward to receive Christ. The priest was glowering.

After that, I began to pray for the sick. "Lord," I said, "in the name of Jesus, I command every affliction to leave every sick person in this tent!" Immediately, the power of God came down and a great number of people stood and began praising God for healing their bodies. Some received their hearing. Others, who had been crippled, were leaping for joy. As the Lord's power swept through that tent, suddenly I saw that big man to my left turn away as though he was terrified at something. Frantically pushing his way out through the crowd, he ran off into the night. No sooner had he left, then I saw the priest leave also.

"Lord, what's going on here?" I said within myself.

"They're probably going to get their guns," another voice suggested.

"No," I thought, "that man was frightened. Something strange happened over there. He won't be back."

When I visited with Bobby later that night, he was as mystified as I was about what had taken place. We talked about it until late in the night.

"They'll not give up easily," Bobby warned. "We're being watched constantly."

The next night the crowd was even larger than the one the night before. I expected to see the priest again (with a new "helper"); but if he was there, I couldn't spot him.

To my dismay, however, there was that same big Hindu man who'd been standing in the left doorway the night before—only this time he was inside the tent.

"Lord," I prayed under my breath, "why'd You let him come back?" I thought about going down and asking him to leave, but that too could be dangerous if he was armed. So I decided it was the better part of wisdom to proceed with the service as I had the night before.

After some singing, I asked for testimonies from the congregation. The big Hindu leaped to his feet.

"Duck! It's a trick!" Bobby whispered.

I braced myself, ready to drop behind the pulpit the moment he reached for his gun. For a fleeting moment, time stood still.

Finally the man spoke. *"Praise the Lord!"* he shouted. "I'm healed!"

My heart turned to water. I almost fainted on the spot. Completely speechless, I just stood there and worshipped the Lord in tongues.

185

"I'm completely healed," the man went on. "Last night I came to your meeting with evil intent. But as you were praying for the sick, the power of God came upon me, and I am now completely well!"

I looked at that man in amazement. "What was your trouble, fellow?"

"I have had terrible abscesses for a long time," he replied. "They were very painful. But last night, as I was standing in the back door of this tent, I felt the power of your Jesus, and I felt those abscesses break."

"Come up here," I said. "I want everyone to hear this testimony." Quickly, he made his way to the front of the tent.

"Now what happened when those abscesses broke?" I asked with great interest.

"I went home," he replied. "I was frightened at this strange feeling of those abscesses breaking open."

"And what did you find when you got home?"

"I found a great deal of blood and pus. It was all over my underclothing. But all the pain was gone. So today I went to the company doctor at the sugar factory where I work, and asked to be examined. And miracle of miracles—he told me the abscesses are completely healed up!"

I can hardly describe what took place from then on. People began to weep and praise God all over that tent. Bobby and I put our arms around that big Hindu and led him to Christ right then and there. And before the service was out that night, seventeen Hindu families were saved. I was a long time getting over that service! In fact, even after we finally got back to Cape Town, Joyce and I continued to talk about it, and we felt a strange sense of tenderness in our spirits for days.

CHAPTER SEVENTEEN

"BUT, LORD, THIS IS UNREASONABLE!"

In 1960, I received a great many invitations to return to America to speak at various conventions and churches. Gathering this to be God's will, I prepared to leave my family once again, with some natural sadness.

"Don't forget to call us," Joyce said at the airport. "I need to hear a man's voice around the house now and then."

"I couldn't forget," I assured her. Then turning to the kids, I said, "Now you be sure and mind Mother, and pray for me every day, will you?"

"We will!" they chorused. And I gave them all a big hug and kiss, and ran for my plane.

When I arrived in the States, it was one steady round of activity as I moved from one city to another, speaking everywhere from large convention halls to little living room prayer meetings.

One of the stops I made was in Lebanon, Ohio. While there, I stayed in the home of Blaine Amburgy, about seven miles out of town. Blaine is one of the international directors of the Full Gospel Businessmen's Fellowship International, and I was to speak in the church he attends the next day.

Since it was Saturday, Blaine and his wife, Helen, thought I'd appreciate a little quietness. "We're going into town to take care of some business

187

matters," Blaine said. "We'll be back shortly, so why don't you just relax a little until we get back?"

"There's plenty of food in the refrigerator, if you get hungry," Helen added.

"Okay," I said. "Sounds good to me."

After they left, I settled down to some Bible study and prayer, trying to get myself prepared for Sunday's ministry. My method of preparation is always the same. I simply ask God to guide me to the passage of scripture I am to talk about. Then I read and re-read that passage until I am sure I thoroughly understand it. This, plus fervent prayer for God's anointing on the ministry of that passage, usually brings results.

So I spent the whole morning in that way: reading, praying for understanding, re-reading, praying for deeper understanding, re-reading again.

Apparently Blaine and his wife were detained; by noon they still hadn't returned, and I was beginning to get hungry. So I got out some lunch meat and made myself a sandwich.

By mid-afternoon, time was growing a little heavy on my hands. I read the newspaper and kept looking out the window, wishing they'd soon get back. "They can't be much longer," I thought to myself. "They said they'd be back shortly."

Just then the telephone rang. I started to get up, when I realized it wasn't Blaine's ring. (He was on a party line.)

When it rang the second time, I just ignored it. But on the third ring, I received a strong impression to pick up the receiver. To my natural mind, this seemed like an unreasonable thing to do; nevertheless I jumped out of the chair and took the receiver off the hook, placing it to my ear. On the other end of the line I heard a very tearful woman.

"Betty," she said, "I've got terrible news about dear Brother George!"

"Oh, my!" the other woman said. "What's wrong?"

"He's in the Dayton General Hospital," she replied. "They've found a tumor on his brain."

"Oh, no!" the other one wailed. "Is it malignant?"

"Yes. They say there's nothing they can do for him!" At that, her voice cracked and she began to sob heavily.

Immediately I knew why God had wanted me to pick up that phone. I held the receiver in my trembling hands, knowing I must minister to this broken-hearted woman.

"Ma'am," I interrupted, "excuse me, I know I shouldn't be listening to your conversation, but I just had the strangest impression to pick up this receiver. May I pray for Brother George?"

"But who are you?" the woman asked in bewilderment, as she sniffed away her tears.

"My name is Robert Thom," I replied. "I'm a friend of Blaine Amburgy's."

"Oh!" she exclaimed. "Are you that man from South Africa who prays for the sick?"

"Yes, ma'am, I'm the man."

"Betty," she said, "isn't this wonderful? Why can't all three of us agree in prayer for Brother George right now?"

So we did. I prayed a simple prayer of faith for this man I didn't even know, asking God to remove that tumor in Jesus' name, while they agreed with me with many Amens and Praise the Lords.

189

When I hung up the receiver, I chuckled to myself. "What a strange prayer meeting *that* was!" I thought. "I wonder what the outcome will be?"

Another voice said, "Sometimes you do the most stupid things. . . ."

When Blaine and Helen came home later that afternoon, I told them all about it. They were quite amused, but promised me they'd let me know if they heard any news about Brother George.

Three weeks later, I was in another town when I received a call from Blaine.

"You know that woman you prayed with on the phone a few weeks ago?" he said.

"Yes. What about her?"

"She came to church this evening and testified about your praying for Brother George. I just thought you'd like to know that when the doctors re-examined him, they couldn't find any trace of the tumor."

"Praise the Lord!" I said. "Isn't that fantastic?"

When I hung up the receiver, I was glad I had obeyed the gentle prompting of the Holy Spirit. I was seeing more and more clearly the importance of stepping out in faith and doing all that God asked of me, no matter how foolish it might seem.

By the middle of September, I finished up my speaking tour and went to New York City, expecting to leave shortly for London, and then southward to Cape Town.

I was staying in the Hotel New Yorker on what was presumably my last day in New York, when I received a phone call from a woman who was the leader of a women's prayer group in a Presbyterian church in Jamaica, New York. She wanted to know if I would come out and speak to her group the next day.

"Well, Lord," I thought, "I've got my plans all made to leave here tomorrow, but if this is what You want, I'll postpone my flight for a day."

So I thanked the woman for the invitation and promised her I'd be there.

When I arrived at the church the next day, I found a group of about thirty women who wanted to know all about the baptism in the Holy Spirit. Seldom have I seen a group of people so eager to hear the Word of God! For well over an hour, I taught them as simply and plainly as I could. Then I offered to pray for those who wanted to have this deeper relationship with Jesus. To my amazement, almost every one of those thirty women received the baptism that day and spoke in other tongues!

As I was leaving the church, a woman said to me, "Reverend Thom, would you be willing to meet a gentleman tomorrow who wants to know more about the Holy Spirit?"

"But, Lord," I wailed inwardly, "I've already postponed my flight once! Surely You don't expect me to wait *another* day!" I was eager to get home, and really didn't see any sensible reason why I should keep postponing my trip.

But then I quickly recalled the lesson God had taught me again and again—that *the life of faith often involves the doing of things that seem completely unreasonable.*

After a long pause, I said to the woman, "What's his name?"

"John Sherrill. Do you know him?"

"I don't think so. Who is he?"

"He's the senior editor for *Guideposts* magazine.

I've already told him about you, and he'd love to talk with you."

"All right," I replied. "I'll postpone my flight another day. This sounds interesting."

"He'll confirm the meeting with you in the morning," she went on. "Where are you staying, and what's the room number?"

"I'm staying at the Hotel New Yorker," I replied, and I gave her my number.

"Thank you," she replied. "You'll hear from Mr. Sherrill in the morning." I went back to the hotel, wondering what new adventure God was leading me into.

The next morning, the phone rang. I answered eagerly.

"Hello. Robert Thom here."

"Mr. Thom, this is John Sherrill—*Guideposts* magazine."

"Yes, Mr. Sherrill—I've been expecting your call. What can I do for you?"

"Robert, I've been deeply involved in a great deal of research on the Holy Spirit, and on the *baptism* of the Spirit, in particular. I just want to ask, is it convenient for you to see me today in my office?"

"I'd be honored," I replied. "What time shall I come?"

"What about noon? I'm working on a rather tight schedule today, but I simply *must* talk with you."

"All right. Where do I come?"

"Three West 29th Street. And, Robert, in view of my position of senior editor, please keep this confidential for the time being. I have no idea how the people here at *Guideposts* will react to my interest in this subject. I'll explain it all to them later."

"I understand," I replied. "I'll see you at noon."

It was exactly twelve o'clock when I walked into John Sherrill's office. He welcomed me warmly, closed the door and immediately began to quiz me about the baptism in the Holy Spirit. How long had I had the experience? What was it like? What had it done for me? What about speaking in tongues? Can you turn it on and turn it off at will? What about the gifts of the Holy Spirit?

By one o'clock, he was still going strong. Glancing at his watch, he said, "Reverend Thom, I don't want this conversation to terminate yet; will you go out and have lunch with me?"

"All right," I said. "I'd be glad to."

So we went out to a restaurant and continued our discussion.

"You know," he said, "I've talked to many interesting people about this experience. In fact, it wasn't so long ago that I interviewed David du-Plessis. Do you know David?"

"Oh yes, very well."

"He's got a beautiful story, hasn't he?"

"Yes, God has used him mightily."

Then he began with the questions again. Is everyone supposed to speak in tongues? What about interpretation—how does it work? Did I ever interpret?

By the time we finished lunch, he was still greatly interested. "Why don't you come back up to the office with me?" he suggested. "Do you have time?"

"Sure," I replied. So we went back up to the office and talked until three that afternoon. Before I left his office, he said with childlike simplicity, "Reverend Thom, will you pray for me before you leave?"

So we bowed our heads, and I felt the mighty presence of the Holy Spirit in that office as we prayed together. I knew God was going to do something unusual in the life of this man, but I had no idea that this was the very John Sherrill who would receive the baptism in the Spirit some two and a half months later, and who would go on to write that beautiful book, *They Speak with Other Tongues*, which has been the means of so many people's receiving the fullness of the Holy Spirit.

When I got back to Cape Town, I had a jolly time of reunion with the family, and talked for hours on end about the many highlights of my trip.

That evening Joyce said to me, "Bob, your mother's been asking about you. I think you ought to go over and see her tomorrow."

"Okay," I said. "She'd probably like to hear all about the trip."

So the next day I drove out to Brooklyn, where my mother had moved. "Lord," I prayed under my breath, "just make me a blessing to her."

As soon as I saw her, I gave her a warm hug and began to tell her all about the many places I'd preached during my tour of the States, and the miracles I'd seen. She listened quietly for a long time. Finally she said, "Bob, God's been very good to you. I'd love to hear more."

"Well, Ma," I said, "why don't you let me take to the Mission tomorrow night to hear me preach? I'll be telling all about my trip."

"All right," she said, "I'll just do that. A little church never hurt anybody."

Sure enough, she was in the service the next

night. God's Spirit came mightily upon me as I told about the many miracles I'd seen; and that night my mother realized she wasn't saved and came forward, at the age of seventy-two, to receive Jesus as her personal Savior. I marveled at the working of the Holy Spirit in her life.

From that time on, I watched her blossom out in faith and obedience. Where once she thought Joyce and I were completely foolish to live as we did, now she too began to launch out in little "unreasonable" acts of faith—but it all made a lot of sense to her now.

"After all," she observed, "God's ways are higher than our ways, and His ideas make a lot more *sense* than ours, don't they?"

CHAPTER EIGHTEEN

LIVING AND DYING BY FAITH

Throughout the sixties, I was constantly on the move, like the coming and going of the ocean tides. Again and again, I was "swept" across the sea to America where I could raise sufficient funds to finance our operation in Africa. Then I'd come back to buy the books and tapes which were so necessary to our work of evangelism.

Some of my friends thought my trips were a little strange, since they were usually spur-of-the-moment ventures with little advance planning. But I'd learned not to expect people to understand this unpredictable faith-life to which I'd committed myself.

Many times God would tell me to go on a speaking tour, and He'd even show me where to stop—but often He'd tell me too late to let my friends know I was coming! So I'd hold my breath and drop in on them by surprise, having faith that God had directed me. Interestingly, it usually turned out that He had!

But in the natural everything was uncertain. Sometimes I had good transportation; at other times I'd hitchhike or ride on buses. Sometimes I spoke to thousands; at other times there were only a handful.

But in all this haphazard coming and going, which seemed like sheer madness, God directed me to people who needed my ministry and people who wanted to help me with my work in Africa.

As long as I kept God and His work first in my life, I marveled at how He opened the windows of heaven and provided the money for this otherwise unsupported ministry. We had no denomination or organization behind us, no mailing lists, no advertising programs; and yet God saw to it that I received every penny needed for our African outreach.

Sometimes God would give me my largest offerings in the smallest meetings. I'd end up with money stuffed in my wallet, in my pockets, and even in the little front pocket of my jacket!

When I'd get back to my room after the services, I would say, "Thank you, Lord, for these American dollars! Just let me be wise in investing this money in Your work!"

I'll confess, though, that sometimes it seemed terribly strange to have that much money, and yet often be hitchhiking from place to place. But I had made up my mind that money designated for our ministry in Africa was never to be used selfishly. God would take care of my personal needs in other ways.

Sometimes the devil tormented me about the risk of living by faith. "You fool!" he'd say. "When you die, there won't be enough money to bury you!"

And I admit that there were times when I found myself wondering about that. I had no insurance, no hospitalization, no pension-fund, and no money in the bank. Sometimes I'd say to myself, "It's all right *living* by faith, but I wonder what it'll be like to *die* by faith?"

In His own peculiar way, God soon let me know the answer to that question. . . .

I was eager to get off the plane in Cape Town after another fruitful trip to the States. As soon as Joyce picked me up, I began telling her about what a great time I'd had, about the many people who'd been saved and filled with the Spirit, and about the generous offerings I'd received for our ministry. I babbled on and on, and I guess I was so full of joy that she hated to tell me the bit of sad news she had for me.

"Bob," she said finally, "you lost a good friend while you were away—"

"Oh? Who?"

"Bosworth."

"Bosworth? My old buddy?"

"Yes, I received a letter from Sister Bosworth. He was in his eighties."

"But when did it happen?"

"About a month ago. She tried to contact you, but wasn't able."

"I can't believe it," I sighed. "Bosworth—gone!"

"Sister Bosworth wants you to stop by and see her the next time you're in the States."

"I'll be making another trip in a few months," I replied. "I just can't get over it—Bosworth! The dean of divine healers! Gone on to glory!"

"It's a big loss to us," Joyce commented, glancing heavenward, "but I'll bet he's having himself a time up there!"

"Yes," I sighed, "a better time than any of us have ever dreamed of."

The next time I was in the States, I travelled down to Coral Gables to talk with Mrs. Bosworth. All the way down, I kept wondering what it had been like for him in those last hours. This man who had won a million souls to Christ and had ministered healing to thousands upon thousands—how does a man like that die?

If I expected to find Sister Bosworth heartbroken and grieving, I couldn't have been more mistaken. "Tommy," she said, "you should have been here; it was glorious!"

"Tell me what happened."

"Well, as you know, he had been bedfast for a year or so. Not that he was sick. He was just old and weary."

"I know," I replied. "He was hardly sick a day in his life."

"That's right," she agreed. "And he wasn't sick the day he died either. But the strangest thing happened. I walked into his bedroom and there he was lying with both hands lifted to heaven. And he'd wave toward heaven with one hand and say, 'Why, helloooooo, Sister Katherine!' I suppose you've heard him talk about Katherine."

"Yes, that's the woman who died a good many years ago."

"Twenty years. And then he'd wave the other hand, and he'd say, 'Hello, Brother Jim Wilson! How are you?' You didn't know Jim, did you?"

"No."

"He died about fifteen years ago. And he just kept waving at people who'd been our bosom friends, and calling their names."

"He must have been getting a glimpse into heaven," I said.

"He *was*. And he was so happy and excited that he didn't even notice me standing there. He just seemed to be completely absorbed in something that couldn't be seen with the natural eye."

"Have you told anyone else about this?"

"A few. Some thought he might have been having hallucinations, but I don't believe that for a minute. Why, he was as sharp and bright as could be."

"Well, some people just don't understand these things."

"Yes, how true. Isn't it sad? Well, I haven't told you the best part yet. He finally sat up in bed and squared his shoulders like a soldier, and said in a strong voice, 'I have fought the good fight of faith! I have run the race! I have kept the faith!' And then, drawing in a big breath, he shouted, *Hal-le-lu-jah!* And instantly he fell back on his pillow, the breath left his body, and he was gone!" At that, she covered her eyes with her handkerchief and wept for joy.

I jumped up off my chair and lifted my hands to heaven. "Hallelujah!" I sobbed. "Isn't that wonderful? What a way to go!"

That evening about sunset, I hitchhiked out to the ocean and watched the tireless waves somersaulting on the beach. As the red sun went down, I couldn't help but praise God for the life and ministry of F. F. Bosworth. I thought I could almost see him out far beyond the shimmering horizon, waving at me in triumph. I could almost hear him saying, "God will never fail you, Robert. Don't ever give up the life of faith. Living by faith is beautiful, and dying by faith is oh, so easy!"

Then I remembered him as I had first seen him in that great revival at Johannesburg. The sound of the slapping waves receded as I found myself sitting again in Maranatha Park Auditorium, listening to the kindly old evangelist preaching the Word of God.

"Lord," I prayed after a long silence, "when it comes time for me to cross over to Your Kingdom, let me go as victoriously as he did!" I wiped some gathering tears from my eyes and recalled a verse of Tennyson's *Crossing the Bar*:

> Sunset and evening star,
>   And one clear call for me!
> And may there be no moaning of the bar,
>   When I put out to sea. . . .

CHAPTER NINETEEN

DESPISE NOT PROPHESYINGS

Throughout several years, I had been noticing the increasing frequency of a new phenomenon in my ministry. More and more I found myself telling individuals and groups things that seemed preposterous—and yet miraculously came true.

At first it frightened me. I would be sitting at a table at a restaurant talking to a friend, and suddenly I would "see" something about that friend that I never knew before. It would be so plain that it was almost like looking into a television picture. I would "see" that my friend was to start a certain kind of business or buy a certain piece of land. And I would feel impelled to tell him what I saw.

After being bold enough to "prophesy" in this way several times, I began to say to myself, "Thom, you'd better be careful. This is scary business, you know. What if you were to be wrong? Somebody might sue you."

Still, my mind would go back to the day I was baptized in the Spirit in McQuade's house, and I remembered so clearly how I'd heard Jesus say, "I give you the gift of prophecy." So, from time to time I would receive unusual revelations about certain people, and I felt I had to be obedient and have enough faith to tell them what God wanted them to know.

The more I allowed God to work through me in this way, the more I began to learn about prophecy. First of all, I learned the absolute necessity of God's anointing. There were times when I would sense an "inrush" of the Holy Spirit, and I'd feel empowered to speak prophetically. The words would flow out of my mouth easily as I yielded to the moving of the Spirit. That was speaking under the anointing.

But there were other times when people would come to me, *asking* for a word from the Lord. They didn't understand the importance of the anointing. I would have to remind them that "prophecy came not in old time by the will of man: but holy men of God spake *as they were moved by the Holy Ghost*" (2 Peter 1:21).

I remember one time when I was rooming with a Christian man in a hotel in Sweden; he kept asking me if I didn't have a message from God for him.

"No," I said. "God hasn't told me anything about you."

But he kept pestering me. He even offered me a $2,000 check if I'd prophesy to him—and that check looked mighty tempting, because I was broke! But I knew I dared not speak without God's anointing, so I kept refusing him.

Then one night, God showed me why that man was so insistent. He was having marriage troubles. He wanted me to tell him to divorce his wife. When I saw his wicked intent, I determined to continue resisting him.

But he'd wake me up in the middle of the night and say, "Did God say anything to you about me yet?"

"No, sir," I replied. "Go back to bed."

The next night he'd wake me up again. "Didn't God tell you anything about my wife?"

"No, sir," I said firmly. "Why don't you give up this foolish business? I know what you want—but you can't buy me off. I only speak when God tells me to speak." So he finally gave up, much to my relief; and I praised God for letting me see the importance of the anointing.

Another thing I learned about prophecy was the importance of testing it out. Whenever I spoke to anyone prophetically, I would instruct them to proceed cautiously. I still believe that no one should rush headlong into some course of action just because someone has prophesied that he should. The Bible tells us very plainly, "Beloved, believe not every spirit, but try the spirits whether they are of God: because many false prophets are gone out into the world" (1 John 4:1). By patiently waiting on God in prayer and quietly observing circumstances, we can discern when a particular prophecy is to be fulfilled—if it is to be fulfilled at all.

During the sixties, I returned to the States and made a stop in Lebanon, Ohio, again staying in Blaine Amburgy's home. While I was there, I had an experience which taught me another lesson about the prophetic ministry: the importance of careful consideration and Spirit-led obedience on the part of the hearer.

Blaine and I were having dinner one evening at the Golden Lamb Hotel. During the course of the conversation, Blaine began to tell me about a certain tract of land he was interested in purchasing. The property looked to him like a good investment, yet he wasn't sure.

As he talked, I "saw" in the Spirit that God

wanted to pour out a great financial blessing on Blaine, and I also understood how this blessing was to come: he was to purchase this property for a bargain price. Later on, that property would become very valuable and could be sold at great profit.

As always, I trembled within at the thought of giving Blaine this message. I felt sure it was a revelation from God, but the question kept going through my mind, "What if you're wrong? What if you're wrong?"

But finally, I knew I had to step out in faith and obey. "Blaine," I said, drawing in a deep breath, "the Lord wants you to buy that land. He wants to mightily bless you, and if you'll buy the property and be patient, you'll see that land skyrocket in value."

"But how do you know that?" Blaine asked.

"I can't tell you how I know," I replied. "I just 'see' it in my spirit, and I'm convinced it's true. You'll miss a great blessing if you don't buy it."

"Well," he said finally, "what do you think I should do?"

"God told me you're to offer the owner $1,000 option money," I replied.

"And then what?"

"That's all God told me," I said. "You pray about it, and if it seems right, then do it."

So that's what Blaine did. He knew he dared not do anything rash or foolish just because a prophecy had been given. He had heard more than enough of so-called "prophecies," and had seen the sad results when gullible people had acted foolishly, ending up in much confusion. Yet he also knew he couldn't deny the value of a genuine prophetic ministry, since the Bible says very plainly in 1 Thessalonians

5:20 that we are not to despise prophesyings. So the thing to do was pray. After all, he *had* been thinking about buying this land anyway, so maybe my prophetic words were God's confirmation that this was His will.

He prayed and prayed for wisdom. In fact, for several weeks afterward, he kept asking God for guidance. He searched the Scriptures and fasted, trying to make a decision.

A few weeks later, I went to see Blaine again. "Let's go down and take a look at that property," I suggested. "I'd like to see it."

So we drove down, and there was this eighty-acre farm. Here and there I could see signs of construction going on along the edges of the property.

"What's going on out there?" I asked Blaine.

"Two new highways are coming through," he explained. "Interstate 71 and State Highway 48. They'll pass right by this tract of land."

I grinned to myself. Maybe this was why God had said the property would become valuable!

As I was looking around, I again "saw" something in the Spirit. Adjacent to the property, a factory was to be built, and God told me it was to be a multi-million-dollar project.

"A multi-million-dollar factory!" I exclaimed within myself.

"*Yes*," the Lord said, "*that is one reason this property will yield great prosperity to him who buys it.*"

So I said to Blaine, "You'd better get your option money ready. There's a multi-million-dollar factory going up right over there, and this property is going to be worth having."

"How do you know that?" he inquired.

"God told me," I replied with a smile.

He just looked at me helplessly, as though to say, "I wish I were as sure about that as *you* are."

When we got back to Blaine's house, he, his wife and I continued to pray together for direction. Finally Blaine said, "Well, I think I'll offer the owner a thousand like you said, and we'll see what happens." So the next day, Blaine went over to discuss the purchase of the property with the farmer who owned it.

"I'd like to put a thousand dollars' option money on this property," Blaine said to him, "that is, if the price is right. What're you asking?"

"Ninety thousand," the man replied. "And that's a real bargain!"

"It sure is!" Blaine exclaimed.

Three days later, Blaine drew up an option which stated that he would purchase the ground if he could arrange adequate financing, and if all other details could be worked out properly.

The actual purchase was closed on April 15, 1965. I had no idea what would happen from that point on, other than the sketchy information I had "seen" in the Spirit. But as time went by, and I stopped in to see Blaine from year to year, I began to marvel at how the prophecy began to take on flesh and bone.

In the first place, construction of the new Interstate 71 and State Highway 48 was due to be finished within a few months, creating an important interchange. That automatically made the property more valuable.

Then Blaine was able to negotiate a lease with the Texaco Oil Company for a service station to be built on 7/10 of one acre of the ground. It was a good location for such a business. Blaine built the station and then leased it to Texaco for fifteen years, which gave him a nice rental income.

Two or three years later, the Cincinnati Milling Machine Company announced their intention to build a multi-million-dollar factory going around three sides of Blaine's property. As the factory was being constructed, however, the builders found there wasn't adequate water supply on their land. When they found out there was water on Blaine's property, they made a deal with him for five acres of his land, and paid him $3\frac{1}{2}$ times per acre what he paid for it in the first place—a total of $17,500!

Several years later, the people who own Coney Island Park announced plans to build a new amusement park called King's Island Park at the next interchange south of Blaine's property, toward Cincinnati. This was done, and up went the value of Blaine's property again!

Besides this, Blaine has been paid around $6,000 by the Soil Bank for not planting any crops during the time he's owned the property.

And only recently, Blaine asked an independent appraiser to give him an appraisal on the acreage. He was told that the property was worth about *five times more* than he'd paid for it! (The property hasn't been sold yet, so who knows how much more value it will accumulate before the "golden moment" of sale?)

When I heard that, I said within myself, "Lord, this is Your doing. I only gave Blaine the message You told me to give him—and I guess *anybody* with a little faith could have done that. But thank You, Lord, for Blaine's willingness to consider Your will in this matter, and to obey the leading of Your Spirit. You said the property would increase in value; and thank You, Lord—You've kept Your Word!"

CHAPTER TWENTY

FANTASTIC VOYAGE

It was good to be in London again. I had completed another speaking tour and was eager to get home. I had arranged to visit briefly with a friend, then catch a plane to Cape Town the next day. Since I had no money, however, I decided to mention this to the Lord again.

Shutting myself in my room, I told God about the impossible situation I was facing and how I was depending on Him to make a way for me. All the offerings I'd received from my speaking engagements had already been taken to the bank and sent to South Africa, and I'd used up the offerings which had been given me for my own use.

While I was praying, a strong impression came to me that I was to change my plans. Instead of taking a plane in the morning, I was to go home the next afternoon on a Union Castle Steamship.

"Lord," I objected, "*that* will take two weeks longer!"

"*But My ways are not your ways,*" He replied. "*I have a work for you on that ship, as you will soon see.*"

"All right, Lord," I replied. "You know best." And I lay down on the bed to relax for a while.

For a long time I lay there wondering what assignment God had for me on that ship. Probably it was quite natural for my thoughts to turn to Smith Wigglesworth, the great plumber-preacher whom God had once used, among other things, to bring revival to a passenger ship. I recalled the incident clearly, since it had been related to me shortly after my conversion by Jimmy Salter, Smith Wigglesworth's son-in-law.

Smith had been on a great steamship traveling from Southampton to Capetown. And interestingly enough, I remembered Jimmy telling me that it was a ship owned and operated by the Union Castle Steamship Company. When some of the people learned that they had this famous evangelist aboard, they asked him if he would participate in the ship's concert. Well, one of the world's most indecent things in those days was a ship's concert. Outside the three-mile limit, anything went.

Smith suspected they were up to mischief, since it was well known that he couldn't sing a note and couldn't even pronounce his h's. But he'd been ridiculed before, so he decided to seize the opportunity to do a little witnessing.

"All right," he said, "I'll take part on two conditions: first, that I'm number one on the program, and second, that you allow me to sing."

To this they agreed, and for several days the concert was highly advertised. Everybody laughed and made wisecracks when they heard that Smith Wigglesworth was going to sing.

"I wonder what he's going to sing?" one woman said.

"How about 'oly, 'oly, 'oly?" one guy suggested mischievously.

211

"Yeah, in all flats," another fellow added, to which everybody responded with uproarious laughter.

But finally the night of the concert came, and the great Smith Wigglesworth got up and sang *Tell Me the Story of Jesus* before 1,500 people. The anointing of the Holy Spirit came upon him and he sang as he had never sung before. By the time he was finished, there was a hush over that great crowd, and he started to preach. The power of the Spirit fell upon the people, and Smith Wigglesworth ended up with a revival on board that ship that lasted for the rest of the voyage.

As I lay there thinking about that incident, I prayed, "Lord, could you use *me* like that?"

And God said, "*Tomorrow afternoon you will sail on that ship and I will give you a revival at sea like Smith Wigglesworth's.*"

I glanced at my watch. It was one o'clock in the afternoon. Quickly I ran downstairs, told my friend about my change of plans, and went on over to the office of the Union Castle Steamship Company to see if I could get passage.

I walked into that office without a penny in my pocket. I had to wait in line to see a Mr. Osborne, who was the shipping agent.

"Mr. Osborne," I said when it was my turn, "I want to get on the ship that is sailing out of Southampton tomorrow afternoon for Cape Town. *The Sterling Castle.*"

"Sir," he replied, "I've got 300 people on the waiting list for that ship. I'm afraid there's no hope."

"But just add my name to the list, will you?" I

insisted. "God told me I'd be traveling on that liner."

"But *I* told you, you haven't got a hope!"

"Mr. Osborne," I said with a smile, "I'll be *on* that ship!"

"Never!" he snapped. "There's no way!"

Nevertheless, he reluctantly added my name to the list and mumbled something not too complimentary under his breath.

Just then I heard a voice calling out: "Paging Reverend Robert Thom. Paging Reverend Robert Thom."

I turned to see a tiny fellow walking by who was not more than 4½ feet tall, dressed in the uniform of the British Overseas Cable.

Catching him by the elbow, I said, "*I'm* Reverend Robert Thom."

"Cable for you, sir," he said, handing me an envelope.

"Thank you," I replied with some embarrassment; I didn't even have enough money to tip him.

When I opened the envelope, there, to my astonishment, was a cablegram for $200. It had been sent by some friends in Spencerville, Ohio.

Whirling around to the shipping agent, I said, "Mr. Osborne, what's the fare to South Africa?"

Without batting an eye he said, "Tourist class is $200."

"Well, isn't that amazing?" I exclaimed, shoving the cablegram over the counter. "I just received this cablegram for *that very amount!*"

He picked it up and looked at it over his gold-rimmed glasses. "Hmmm, yes—two hundred dollars," he mumbled.

"Isn't that wonderful?" I gloated. "Those people had no idea I needed this money."

"But this isn't your money," he replied, still studying the cablegram.

"Don't be silly," I replied. "It certainly is."

"I beg your pardon, sir; if you will look more closely, you will see that this cablegram has been made payable to the Union Castle Steamship Company."

Sure enough, when I looked again, I saw that a mistake had been made in the address. Authorization was given to pay $200 to the addressee: Union Castle Steamship Company, c/o Reverend Robert Thom, Bond Street, London, W.C. 1, England.

"You see," the agent pointed out, "legally this money belongs to Union Castle Steamship Company."

"Yes, I see that," I said, "but what are you trying to tell me?"

"Why, simply that this money has got to go through our books and through our bank. I can't pay you this money until I get permission."

"And in the meantime, what am *I* going to do?"

"I don't know, sir, but this money will have to go through the proper channels, and that will take a day or so."

I was stumped. What was I going to do now? I stood there silently for a few moments. Finally I said, "Well, Mr. Osborne, you go ahead and process that cablegram. In the meantime, I'm going down to Southampton. And I'll be on that ship tomorrow afternoon."

"Oh, no you won't!" he spat back.

"Oh, yes I will!" I grinned. "God told me I'll be on that ship."

"You're wasting your time, Mr. Thom," he replied in disgust. "And mine as well. Good day, sir!"

I went back to my friend's home later that afternoon, sure that God was going to unravel the tangled mess and work out His purpose. That evening, my friend told me how much he appreciated my ministry and gave me a few dollars in an envelope. When I counted it out, there was just enough to pay my train fare to Southampton.

So the next day I made the trip south to Southampton, 160 miles away. The ship was due to sail at 4:00 that afternoon. At 2:00, I went into the customs shed and put my bags under the initial "T." In the natural, I knew the voyage was impossible. There was no sign that I would be able to get on that ship. But "faith is the evidence of things not seen," so I went ahead and went through all the motions of being a passenger. Walking over to a table, I began to prepare all the necessary documents to go through the Immigration Authority. As I stood there writing, a security guard came up to me.

"Your name, sir?"

"Reverend Robert Thom," I replied.

"Robert Thom? Boy, have they ever been paging *you* for the last hour!"

"They have?"

"Yes. Take all your stuff and go on board ship to the tourists' lounge. That's where they've been paging you from."

"Thank you, sir!" I replied, gathering up my papers and bags and heading for the gangplank as fast as I could go. When I got out to the ship, there must have been over 300 people waiting to get on board, although there was still an hour before anyone would be permitted on deck.

"Excuse me," I said, elbowing my way through the crowd. "Excuse me, please. . . . I'm sorry, madam . . . . Excuse me, sir. . . ."

I'm sure they must have wondered who I was and what right I had to board that ship before anybody else! When I walked into the tourists' lounge, there was the Purser sitting at a table, filling out some forms.

"Reverend Robert Thom, sir," I said.

"Reverend," he said, "we've been paging you. Where have you been?"

"Well," I said confidently, "it took me a bit of time to get here—but I'm here; what is it?"

"Sir, we've had one cancellation, and for some unknown reason, though you are at the bottom of the waiting list and I know nothing about you, I feel I should give you the berth."

"All right, how much is it?" I asked.

"Two hundred dollars."

"Sir," I said, "I've already deposited the money at your office in London. Will you kindly phone your agent, Mr. Osborne?"

"I will," he said, "but why did you pay in advance when you didn't even have a berth?"

"Mr. Osborne will explain that," I replied.

So while he was placing the call to London, I said under my breath, "Lord, this is wonderful! But there's one more thing: I haven't got any pocket money. I'll be at sea for two weeks, and we'll be crossing the equator, and I can't even buy a bottle

216

of pop. If you don't mind, Lord, could I have one more miracle?"

Just then the Purser hung up the phone. "Everything's clear," he said. "Give me just a moment to make you a receipt, then you can be on your way."

As he started to write, he suddenly stopped and said, "Sir, are you a bona fide Reverend?"

"Yes, sir," I replied.

"Okay," he said, "you get a ten percent discount. I'll just give you back twenty dollars. Is that all right?"

"Praise the Lord!" I said right out loud. He grinned and finished filling out the receipt. A couple of hours later, the big ocean liner put out to sea, and I was on my way home.

After a day or two out on the Atlantic, I began thinking about the promise God had made to give me a revival at sea like Smith Wigglesworth had. So I prayed earnestly for guidance; and on our first Sunday at sea, I was impressed to ask permission to have a service that evening. The Captain was very kind and gave me permission to use the big room where the passengers often gambled and drank. He even had the service announced for me over the P.A. system.

When the time came for the service, so many people crowded into that room we couldn't accommodate them all. So I got permission to open the windows of the room and put out loudspeakers so those on the deck could hear. There were 1,500 people on board that ship, and I was told that about 1,200 turned out for that meeting.

One of the ship's officers presided over the service. After some singing and receiving an offering, I was introduced. I preached about salvation through the blood of Jesus. I experienced a great anointing that night, and when I gave the invitation for men and women to receive Christ, many people came forward and prayed the sinner's prayer.

After the service, the officer handed me the offering.

"Thank you, sir," I said, "but I don't need that." I wanted to be careful lest I give the impression that money was my motive for preaching.

"But this is the speaker's privilege, sir," he replied. "We always give the offering to the speaker."

"I appreciate that," I replied, "but what I have seen tonight in men and women's receiving Christ out here on the Atlantic Ocean more than repays me for any effort I've made."

"That's beautiful," he said, "but under orders of the ship's Purser, I must insist that you take the money."

"All right, give it here," I said. "I'll go talk to the Purser about it."

A minute later, I walked up to the Purser's desk and laid the money down in front of him.

"What's this?" he inquired.

"That's the offering from tonight's service."

"Then it's yours," he replied. "All offerings go to the speaker."

"Mr. Purser," I replied, "I appreciate this very much, but you see, I'm an ex-sailor boy and—"

"Don't tell me!" he interrupted. "*You* were a sailor?"

"Yes, sir," I smiled, "and a very drunken one too. Now would you mind giving this offering of eighty-six British pounds to the Sailors' Orphans and Widows Fund?"

"You don't mean that," he said in disbelief.

"Yes, sir."

"Tell me about yourself."

So I began to witness to that Purser. I told him all about the drunken years in the Navy, and how Jesus had changed my life. I told him about the many miracles I'd seen around the world. He drank in every word, sometimes blinking to hold back a tear.

"Reverend," he said after I'd finished, "I want to do something for you. You know that room where you spoke tonight? I'm giving it to you for the rest of the voyage; you can have services in there every night if you want to."

So that's exactly what I did. For the rest of that voyage, we had revival. By the time we reached Cape Town, I felt like Smith Wigglesworth II.

CHAPTER TWENTY-ONE

205 HENLEY MANOR

The ministry in Africa continued to expand. God had shown me that the natives of the land could be trained to become missionaries much more inexpensively than by bringing in American missionaries. Whereas an American missionary would require several hundred dollars a month to get along on, a native who already knew the language and the local customs could reach his people for as little as $35 a month. So we began adding more and more native evangelists to our staff and sending them out to conduct crusades in many parts of Africa.

I confess I found it difficult to rest in my bed at night when I thought about Africa's 344,000,000 people, mostly without Christ. Communist agents and Mohammedan missionaries by the thousands were busy all over the continent, scattering their literature and proclaiming their message. What right did I have to rest so easily when they were out toiling almost night and day?

My son, Drummond, who had gone to the States and had decided to give his life to the ministry, started an organization in Louisville, Kentucky, for the express purpose of supporting dozens of native evangelists, as well as providing them with Bibles, books, bicycles and P.A. systems. This was a great help to us, and yet there was so much more to be done.

I was also greatly concerned about the spiritual growth of our young converts. God laid on my heart the importance of placing helpful literature in their hands; so I wrote a number of books and pamphlets and printed them by the thousands on our own press. In four months, we printed over 80,000 books in the Afrikaans language and made plans to publish literature in one hundred of the African languages and dialects.

In the midst of all this activity, however, God never let me forget that I also had young Christians to take care of in my own home. While Joyce was a wonderful help in raising the children in a Christian way (and I never could have gotten along without her), still I had *my* obligations too. God expected me to be the spiritual leader of my home. So I was constantly challenged about giving proper amounts of time and attention to Joyce and the few children who still remained at home, while doing God's work at the same time.

I suppose it was this realization of responsibility that made me very ready to accept the Lord's suggestion in 1968 that I take my family on an evangelistic tour of Europe. We had gone on many such tours before, and I was sure it would be good for us again. However, I had not the slightest notion where the money would come from for such an expensive undertaking.

But there *had* to be a way. Joyce was getting more and more restless and kept talking about moving out of our house.

"Bob," she'd say, "I think God wants us to move

out of here. Now that most of the children are grown, there's no need for us to have such a big house anyway."

"But where would we move?" I replied.

"I'd like to live at Henley Manor."

"*Henley Manor?* The fancy apartment building down by the sea?"

"Yes. Wouldn't you like that?"

"I suppose I'd like it, but there's no way we can afford it."

She looked at me in amusement. "Is this Africa's man of faith talking?" she teased. "Or did God die yesterday and nobody told me?"

"But you've got to use common sense," I countered weakly.

"I *am* using common sense," she insisted. "I think Henley Manor would be a much better headquarters for our ministry than this place. And besides, didn't Jesus say, 'What things soever ye desire, when ye pray, believe that ye receive them, and ye shall have them'?"

"Yes, that's what He said," I admitted.

"Well, then, I say that we're soon going to be living in Henley Manor."

"You must be mad!" I replied. "We'll never live there."

"But I say we will," she insisted. "God told me."

Before I went to sleep that night, I pondered the matter more deeply. I *had* to take Joyce and the kids on that trip to Europe. Nothing else would cure this restlessness and those crazy notions about moving. "Lord," I prayed, "You and I both know this trip is financially impossible—but You said, 'What things soever ye desire, when ye pray, believe that ye receive them, and. . . .'" Suddenly I remembered that *that* was the very promise Joyce had quoted to me earlier in the evening! I grinned in the dark and went to sleep.

The next day, I shared my idea about the tour to Europe with the kids. They all "exploded" at once, and wanted to know when we'd be going, how long we'd be gone, if we'd camp in a tent and when we could start packing.

"Hold everything!" I said. "As you know, this is going to cost a lot of money—and we can only do it if God supplies the need. So I'd suggest we do some praying before packing!"

And we did. We prayed earnestly about the matter for a couple of weeks. Finally, God made it clear to me that the trip should be a venture of faith. Instead of waiting until we had enough money, we would take what money we had and go as far as it would take us. Then we'd depend on God to supply the need for the next leg of the journey—and the next—until we finally got back home. I felt this would be a great way to teach the kids more about the joys of living by faith.

We made arrangements to go as far as London first, and then we would cross over into France. We planned to visit many countries, ending our tour in Geneva, Switzerland, and then returning to Cape Town.

"It's winter up north," I warned Joyce, "so there's a possibility we may have to stay in London for a while."

"But where?" Joyce asked. "We'd have to rent a house, wouldn't we?"

"I suppose so," I replied. "I've got an idea. I'll help you pack as many supplies as possible just in case we have to rent. Then I'll fly to London ahead of you and see if I can find a furnished house. You and the kids can come by ship."

That sounded like a good idea to Joyce, so we spent the next two or three days packing supplies.

"Be sure to pack plenty of blankets," I told Joyce. "We don't want anybody catching cold."

We packed seventeen cartons of bedding, dishes, silverware, cutlery, etc., and made plans to have them transported to Southampton on the same ship that Joyce and the kids would be traveling on. Within a few days, I boarded a plane and flew to London, while the family left on a ship that would arrive in London two weeks later.

I had communicated with some Christian friends in London, and shared our plans with them. They had promised to meet me at the airport. And, sure enough, when I stepped out of the plane into the cold, wintry air at Heathrow Airport, there was a good brother there with a station wagon.

"Brother Thom," he said, "I hope you like this station wagon. Our church is donating this to you and your family to use for the duration of your trip through Europe." His breath made little puffs of vapor as he spoke.

I thanked him profusely and then was taken home with him for a few days' stay, until more definite arrangements could be made.

For the next two weeks, I prayed for guidance and looked for houses. But no matter where I looked, I couldn't locate a suitable house. "Well," I thought, "the winter's not all that bad. Maybe we should forget about a house and get on with the tour."

So I drove the station wagon down to Southampton in time to meet Joyce and the kids. When the kids first spotted me as they came down the gang-plank, they all let out a shout and started chattering wildly.

Within a short time, I took them over where I had the station wagon parked. "Look here," I said to Joyce. "We've got transportation!"

"Where'd you get it?" Joyce asked.

"That's miracle number one!" I replied, nudging her gently as she stood there shivering. "It's a gift to us, as long as we're in Europe."

"Praise the Lord!" she exclaimed. "Isn't it amazing how God keeps providing for us?"

"It sure is!" I smiled.

"There's nothing impossible, is there?"

"Absolutely nothing!" I sang out.

"Then not even Henley Manor is impossible—is it?"

I acted as though I didn't hear her, and proceeded to unlock the station wagon doors.

We all hopped into the wagon and drove over to see the shipping agent about arranging storage for our seventeen boxes of supplies, until such a time as we'd need them. I explained to Joyce that I'd had difficulty locating a house.

"Maybe the Lord doesn't want us to rent a house," Joyce replied. "Can't we get on with the tour?"

"I was thinking the same thing," I replied.

But when our friends in London heard about our plans, they thought we ought to wait until spring to go over into Europe. But we prayed earnestly, and finally, through some services we held, we got enough money together to pay for our fare and shipment of the station wagon to France. So we left our supplies in storage and continued on our way.

Once in France, we set out on our journey, and for the next several months that station wagon became our traveling home. Even though the weather was cold, we met many warm-hearted friends who always offered us a cozy place to stay at night. I conducted services in many churches, halls and homes, and many spiritually hungry people were saved, healed and baptized in the Spirit. Both Joyce and the kids thoroughly enjoyed being in the services and helping in whatever ways they could.

The odometer kept rolling up the miles as we moved steadily through the winter wonderland of Belgium, the Netherlands, Germany—on and on, for seemingly endless miles. Always, we received just enough money from the offerings to keep us going to the next stop.

Toward the end of winter, we had completed the circle and were heading back west through the majestic Alps of Switzerland. Upon arrival in Geneva, our trip would be finished. I would take the station wagon back to England, and the family would fly back to South Africa.

When we checked into the Pascal Hotel in Geneva, I said to Joyce, "Let's stay here for the weekend. The trip's been tiring, and it will be a good chance for you and the kids to get out and enjoy the snow." So that's what we did.

By Monday morning we were all rested up, and we prepared to check out of the hotel and drive over to the airport.

A short time later, as we were waiting for the plane, Joyce said to me, "Now don't forget to get our boxes out of storage and get them shipped back to Cape Town. I'll be needing silverware and dishes."

"But what'll you do until they arrive?" I asked.

"Borrow, I suppose. How long will it take?"

"Two or three weeks from the time they get shipped out. They should have been sent two weeks ago. Plus there's the storage bill to pay before I can get the stuff on the boat."

"Oh, dear, I forgot about that. Will it be much?"

"Seventeen packages at thirty-five cents per package per day—that'll come to several hundred dollars, I suppose. Plus shipping costs to Africa."

"But where will you get all that money?"

"I haven't the slightest idea," I admitted, "but God always comes through, doesn't He?"

"Okay," she said, as she gave me a farewell kiss. "I'll see you in a few weeks at Henley Manor."

"Henley Manor!" I replied with a laugh. "I thought you forgot about that! We can't afford to live there; we're poor people, remember?"

"But we've got a rich God!" she replied with a twinkle in her eye. "C'mon, kids, the plane is loading!"

I kissed them all hurriedly, and in a few minutes they were high above Geneva, heading for sunny Cape Town.

When I finally arrived back in London a few days later, I went immediately to the shipping company to see about my seventeen cartons. I hadn't the slightest notion how I'd pay the bill, but God knew how important it was, and I felt sure He'd make a way.

When I walked into the shipping agent's office and inquired about the items in storage, the young clerk behind the desk began filling out a form.

"Your name, sir?"

227

As soon as I mentioned my name, he stopped writing and his face became very pale.

"What's wrong?" I asked.

"Sir," he replied hesitantly, "I'm sorry to tell you, we've made a terrible mistake. Two weeks ago, we sent your packages to Cape Town. They arrive there tomorrow."

"But why did you do this without my instructions?" I demanded.

"I don't know," the poor fellow wailed. "It was just some kind of mistake. I'm sorry, I can't explain it."

"Well, who's going to be financially responsible for all this?" I asked. "What about the storage costs and the shipping costs?"

"Believe me, sir," he replied, "our company will take care of the whole thing. I just don't understand how such a stupid mistake could have happened, but I assure you, it won't cost you a cent. I hope you understand."

Suddenly I did! "Lord!" I said under my breath. "What a miracle!"

Then I said to the agent, "Young man, would you mind putting that in writing—that the company is taking care of this bill? Just give me a signed release, and tell them to leave the goods in Cape Town."

"Yes, sir!" he replied, obviously relieved that I wasn't angry.

As soon as he handed me the release, I rushed to a telephone and called Joyce, who was already back in Cape Town by that time. Was she ever surprised to hear my voice!

"Bob, is anything wrong?" she asked.

"No! Everything's right!" I exclaimed. And I went on to explain to her what had happened. "So all you need to do is go over to the shipping company tomorrow and claim the goods!" I concluded. "Isn't that wonderful?"

"Praise the Lord!" she squealed. "This is a miracle!"

"It sure is!" I agreed.

"Bob," she said, lowering her voice, "can I ask you a question?"

"Sure, what?"

"Can I have those boxes sent over to Henley Manor?"

The timing couldn't have been better. I chuckled and replied, "Honey, if you've got faith for the rent at Henley Manor, then go ahead!"

"Wheeee!" she sang out. "Africa's man of faith finally comes through!" We both laughed until our sides hurt.

When I hung up the receiver, I decided I'd better get home as soon as possible. After a few days, I received enough offerings from additional services to buy my plane ticket home.

As soon as I got off the plane in Cape Town, I called Joyce to come down and get me. In a matter of minutes, she came and drove me to our new home and headquarters at 205 Henley Manor.

CHAPTER TWENTY-TWO

THE ANSWER

In 1970 I was sitting in our apartment reading the newspaper when I came across an item about a certain ex-chaplain who was to be giving his testimony at a church in Durban. The article told how this chaplain had served in World War II with a South African Army unit up in Egypt—at a place called El Kantara.

"El Kantara!" I said to myself. "That's the place where *I* was stationed." Glancing at the man's name again and recognizing it, I nearly leaped out of my chair.

"Joyce!" I shouted. "Look here!"

"What is it?" she asked, stepping into the doorway.

"Look at this newspaper article. Remember that chaplain I told you about who refused to help me up in Egypt when I was having my drinking problem?"

"You mean the one you tried to talk to after you came back from the Holy Land?"

"Yes, that's the one."

"Is that article about him?"

"Yep. Apparently he's gotten saved. He's going to be giving his testimony at a church over in Durban."

"Well, isn't *that* something! Are you going to go over to hear him?"

"I'd like to, but that's quite a long drive. I think I'll write to the old rascal. I wonder if he'll remember me?"

So I got out my pen and paper and began to write. "Chaplain," I began, "I want you to think back to 1942 when you were stationed in the desert at a place called El Kantara. If you will remember, a soldier boy came up to you. It was five o'clock, and the mess hall was just opening, and he wanted to speak to you about his soul. And you said you didn't have time, and you went in to have your drinks.

"Chaplain," I went on, "I am that soldier boy. I saw the news item in the paper about your meeting in Durban, and I just want you to know that I've been saved; I've been converted through the power of Jesus Christ." And I then went on to share with him some of the exciting things that had happened to me since my conversion. Along with the letter, I sent him one of my books.

A few days later, I received a beautiful letter back: "Oh, how I thank God for your salvation!" he said. "You'll never know how that thing troubled me down through all these years. Over and over I'd remember how I failed you in your hour of need, and my conscience would trouble me greatly. I thought I'd never get any relief from that awful burden of guilt—but then your letter came! Oh, how sweet that letter was to my soul! The burden has finally been lifted."

When I showed the letter to Joyce, she said, "You know, Bob, there's never a dull moment when you really trust Jesus, is there?"

"I should say not," I replied. "It's too bad so many people don't understand that. The world is full of people who are searching for excitement and adventure—and here we've had more excitement in a few years of following Jesus than most people have had in a lifetime."

"Well, people get confused," Joyce continued quietly. "The world's bright lights and loud music and glasses of wine make them think that these things must be awfully exciting."

"But we know the new wine is better, don't we?"

"I should say!" she exclaimed. "I wouldn't go back to that old life for all the world's gold!"

"And yet we've had our problems, bringing up nine children without a steady income and never knowing how we're going to pay the rent from one month to the next. Do you realize that last week was the 236th time you've asked me that question, 'How are we going to pay the rent?' "

"There you go again, keeping count!" she laughed. "But the wonderful thing is that we've never been late one single time in all these twenty-one years."

"Well, that's what makes the Christian life exciting," I said. "It's having big problems and watching God solve them in His own way."

"Of course, lots of Christian people don't see the kind of miracles we've seen," she observed. "The churches are full of Christian people who live dull, humdrum lives and hardly ever see a miracle. I wonder why?"

"There's just one answer to that question," I replied. "*Great things will never happen until you're willing to go out on a limb with God.*"

"I guess that seems like too big a risk for some people," she commented.

"I suppose," I said. "But after you learn how completely trustworthy God's Word is, it doesn't seem like a risk anymore."